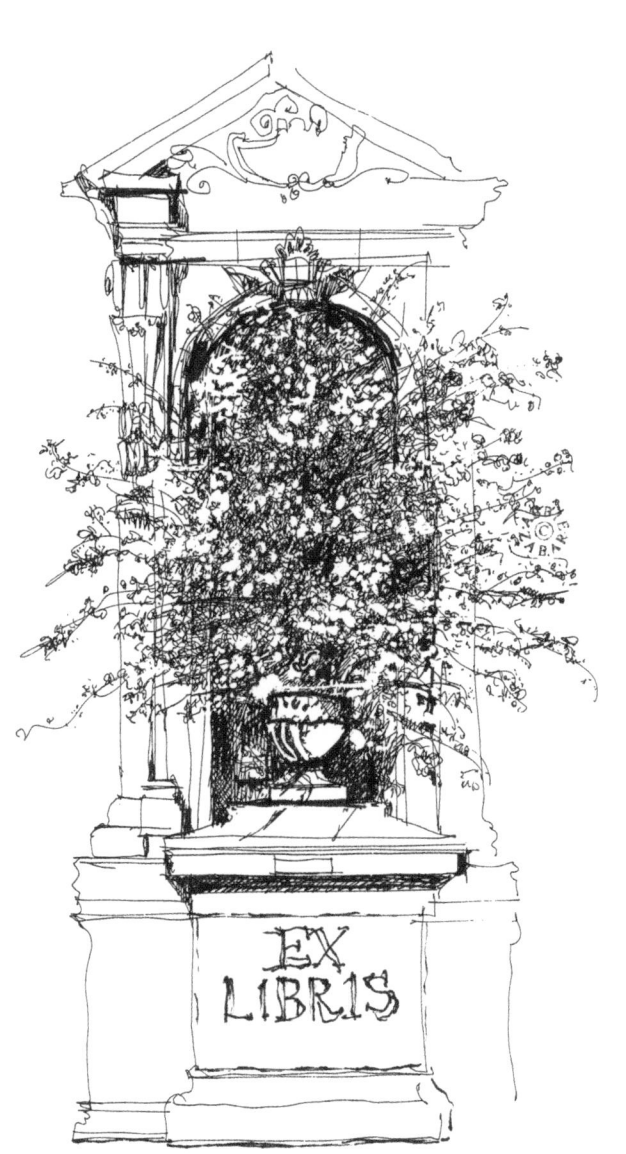

EX LIBRIS

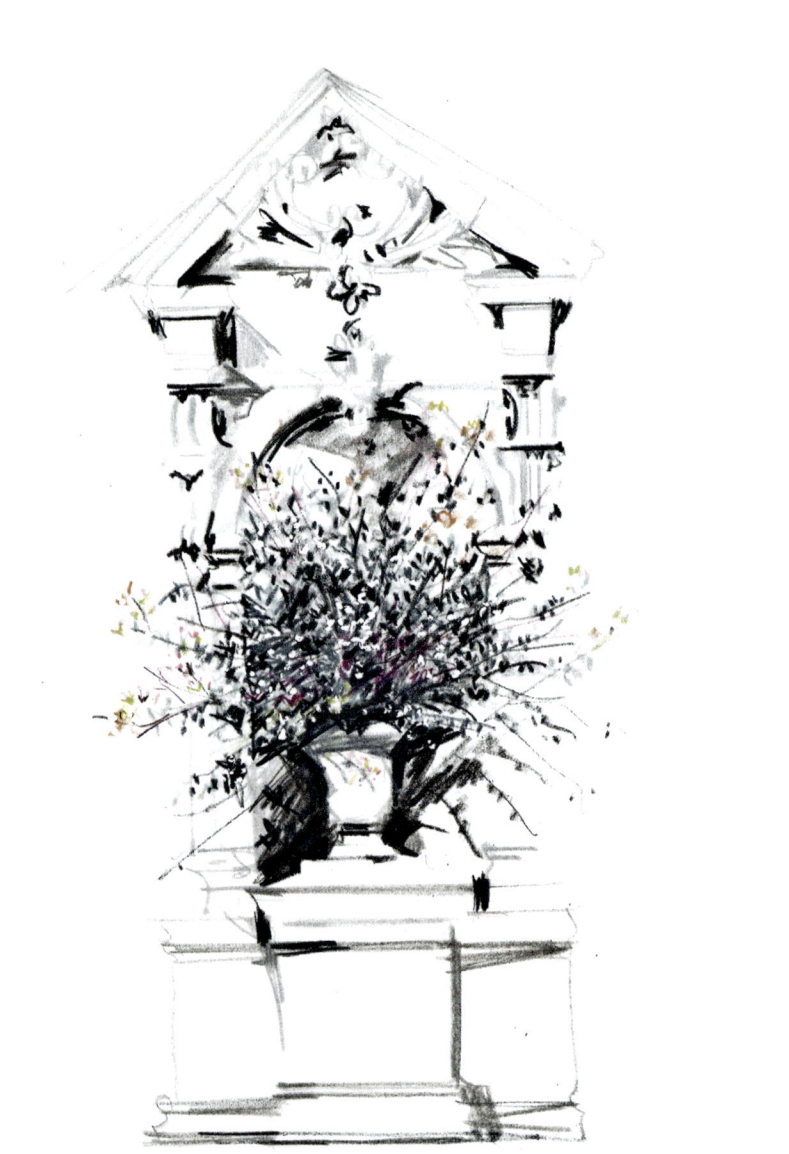

Abbie Zabar

Bouquet

FLORAL ARRANGEMENTS AT THE METROPOLITAN MUSEUM

ACC ART BOOKS

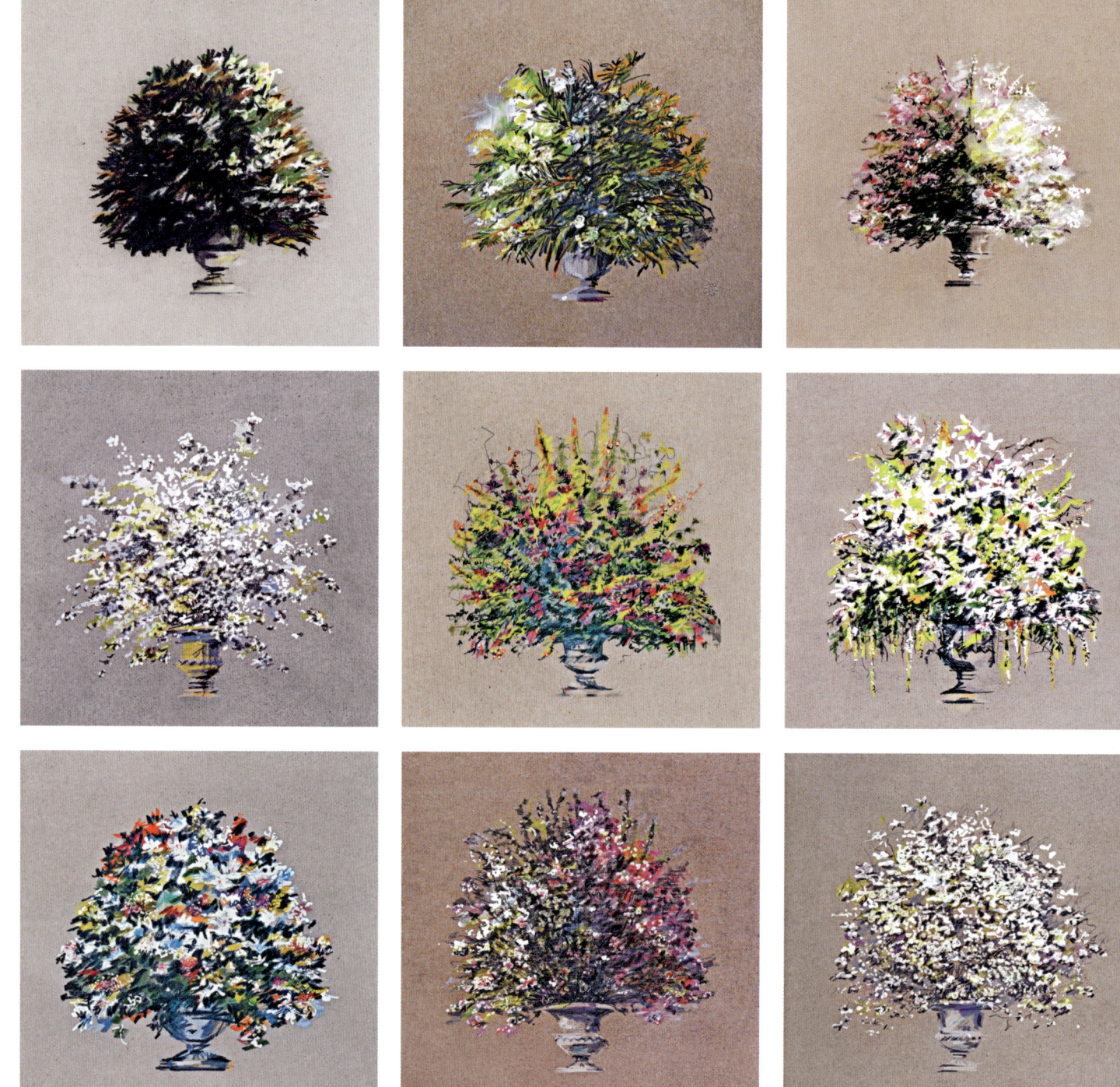

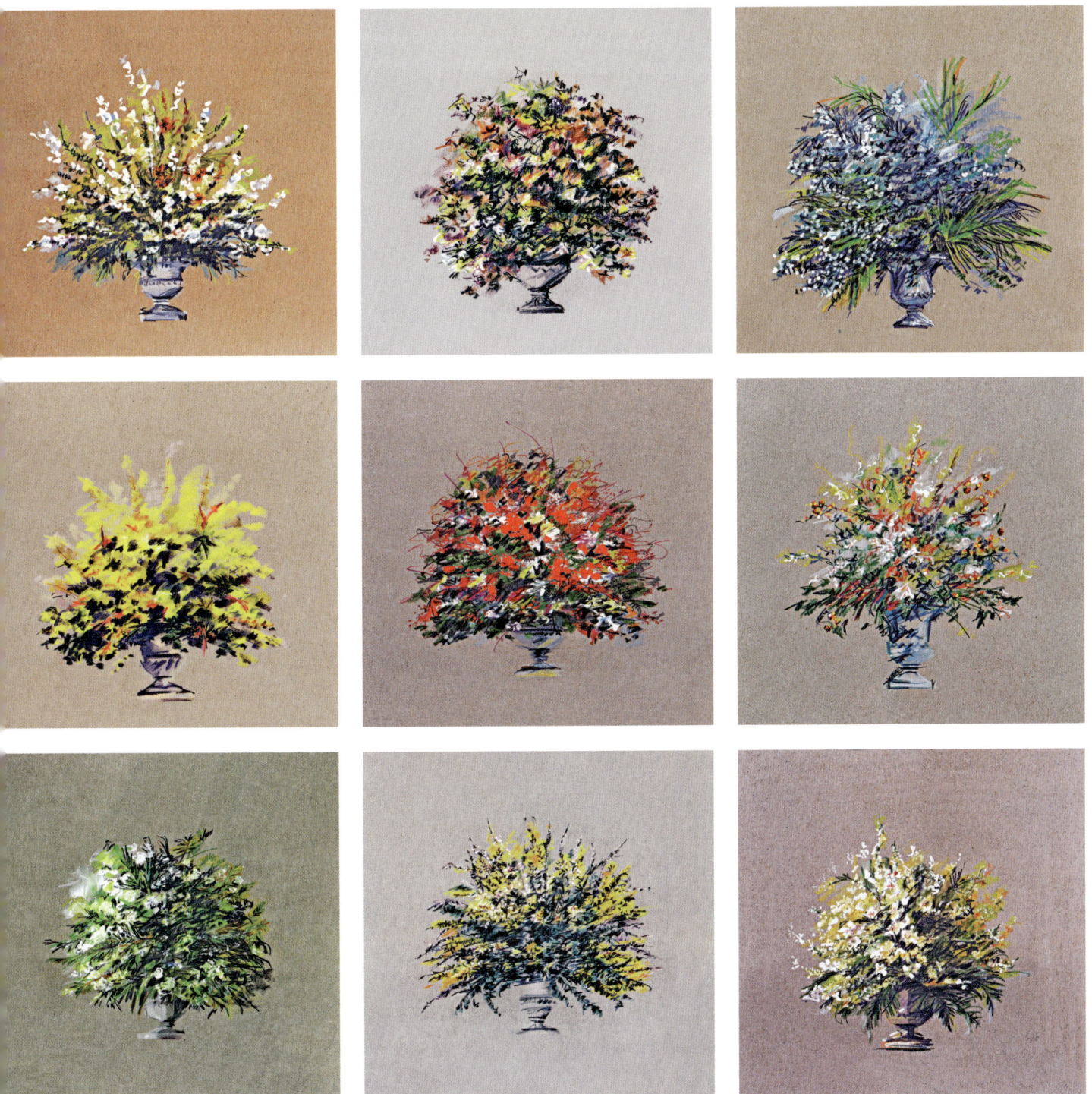

For my mother

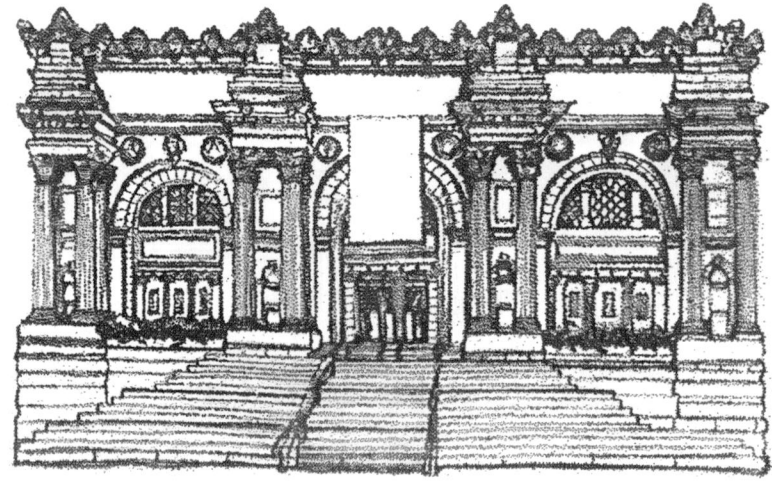

Contents

Foreword

"Sometimes, I would see her there, a little figure in the dark. We passed each other, two ships in the night's sky. Both of us wearing jeans, each focused on flowers in our own way. I would wave to Abbie in the middle of the Great Hall, often sitting, appropriately enough, on one of the small canvas stools that the museum keeps handy in the coat-check area for students when teachers are talking about the Met's collections. She would be surrounded by her pencils, a pad in her lap. Or sometimes in conversation with the guards, figuring out which bouquet was going to be her subject that morning, which arrangement needed to be lit when the Great Hall was still dark. I never stood over her shoulder, nor questioned her judgments. Never asked why she did what she did, why certain floral elements were highlighted, others eliminated.

Anything so perishable as living flowers will eventually be disappointing because they are ephemeral. But Abbie's spontaneous drawings captured the short-lived presence of my bouquets. She has kept their fleeting vitality alive. For her to document my work through her eyes and draw them for over 10 years was a profound compliment."

Chris Giftos, Floral Master at the Metropolitan Museum of Art, 1970–2004

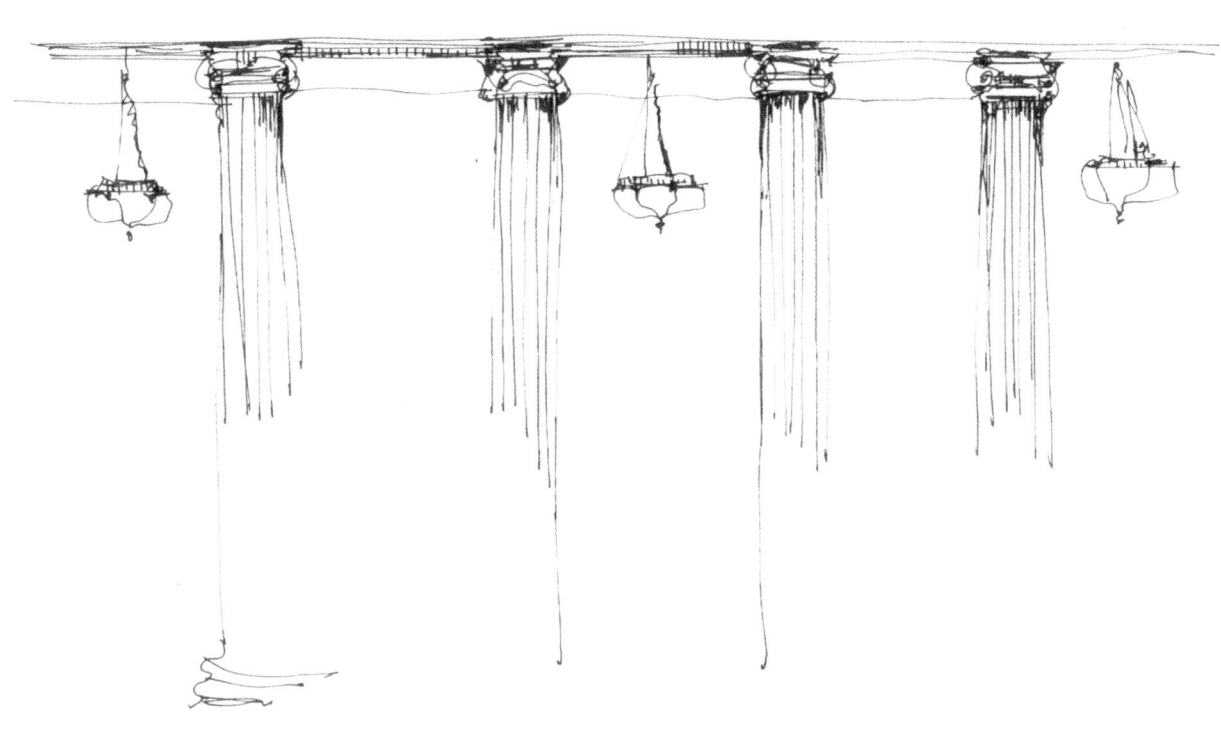

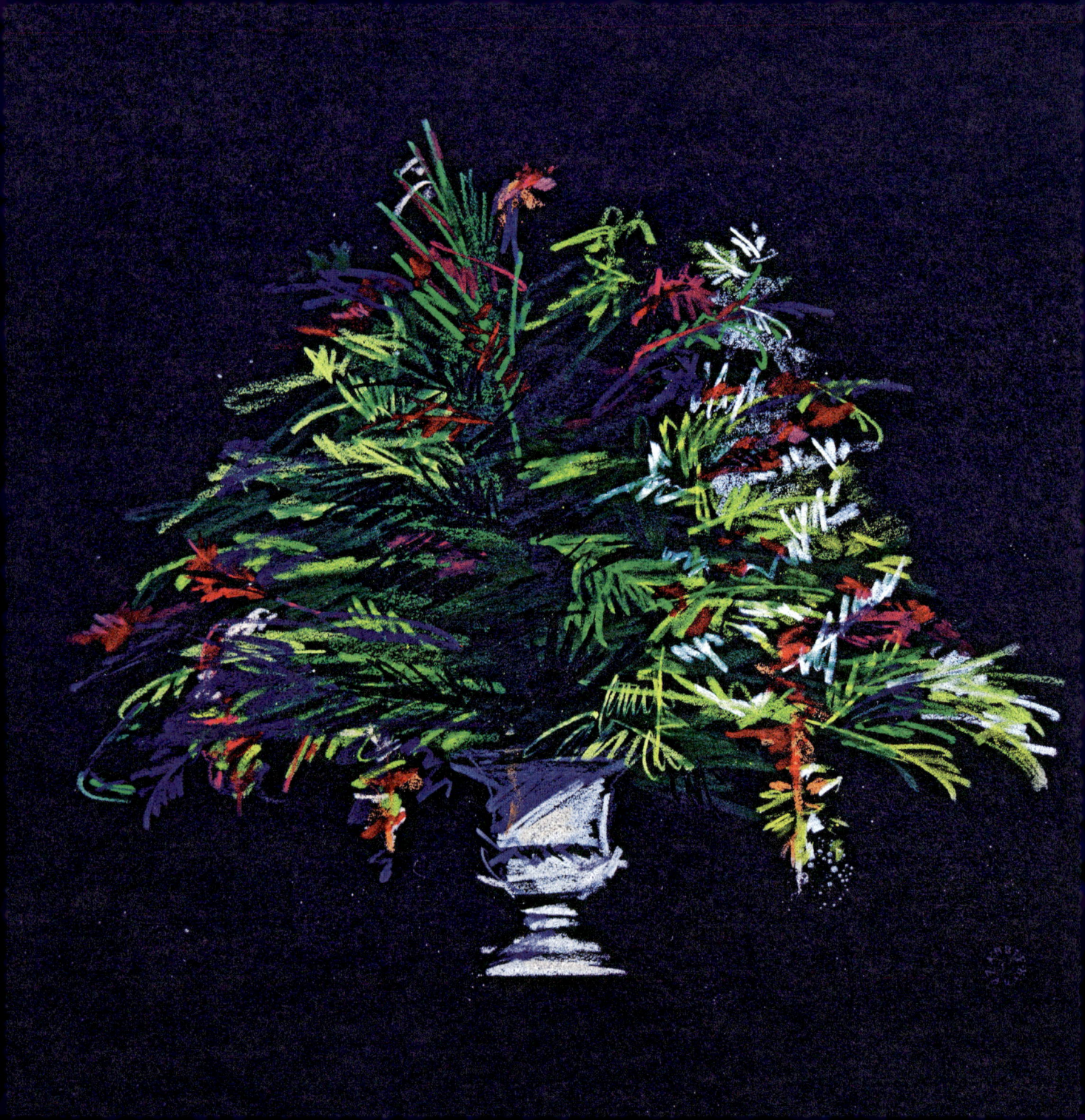

Chapter 1
Drawing in the Dark

I am walking north on Fifth Avenue. A laminated pass issued by Special Events hangs from a chain around my neck. Sheets of cardboard, pads of acid-free paper and a stash of colored pencils bulk up my backpack. No cars or buses are in sight, yet I see pigeons at the base of the wide stone steps, waiting for the food carts, along with early-bird tourists.

It is a quarter to eight on Sunday morning and the midnight guards are finishing their shift. I am grateful that they unlock a single set of doors as soon as they see me—every minute counts. I remind myself to bring them cookies when I start baking for the holidays. I then sign my name on the first line of a pristine new page, as I did for a decade.

The heavy bronze-framed glass doors of the Metropolitan Museum of Art will open to the public at 9:30. I must be finished drawing and packed up before then.

The museum is dark. No spotlights are on. Still, a few rays of sun squeeze through crevices in the clerestory. I've worked with less.

More than seven million visitors a year—14,000 a day and over 20,000 on a holiday—pass into the Great Hall through long, braided ropes hanging from iron stanchions. An orgy of 12-ft-high bouquets herald tourists, regulars, and the seasons with a most enthusiastic "Welcome to the Met." These weekly-changing arrangements are enshrined in niches where visitors might expect to see framed portraits or busts of pooh-bahs, not bouquets reminiscent of the 17th-century Flemish flower paintings in the upstairs galleries. Urns the same neutral color as the surrounding stone walls are filled with curated flowers, leaves, and branches from around the globe and are probably the most famous floral arrangements in the world.

It is as quiet as a church but for the crickets that sneak in on the vines, except when my pencils fall on the marble floor and it sounds like an explosion from a midtown manhole cover. I am using waxy Prismacolor pencils, a humble medium that won't leave a liquid mess.

There are epiphytic orchids from rainforests in Honduras, Hawaiian birds-of-paradise, South African red-hot pokers, and proteas from Provence. The tulips are harvested from bulbs in the Netherlands' sandy soil, in fields that stretch as far as the eye can see. Brilliant yellow forsythia always lights up the Great Hall in February, followed by other forced branches of the pinkest quince and then apple blossoms, blinding in their whiteness. A nose-twitching aroma wafts above the lilies when globes of hydrangeas and endless sunflowers appear in summer. Palm fronds or other giant leaves are filler. The glossy dark foliage of *Magnolia grandiflora* with brown felted backs, plus branches stippled with gleaming red berries and thick stalks of cut amaryllis are a horticultural tip-off that the holidays are coming. As a gardener, I know what to expect.

If I had to name my favorite pickings, it's the anonymous twigs and grasses of local roadsides or brambles from the woods, as championed by Constance Spry, the mid-20th-century contrarian British florist who nevertheless was responsible for the flowers at Queen Elizabeth II's coronation.

Long before those weekends, I was a staff artist for trade dailies. Drawing for a newspaper turned out to be my best art school. Monday to Friday, I was on a deadline. There was no waiting for the muse to hit. Nor time for roughs, comps, or preliminary sketches. My first drawings are always my finals and, even if doodled on the backs of register receipts, my favorites. For five days straight, I worked in a heat. Friday, I got paid. Not a whole lot of money but how many bosses will cut a weekly check for someone who wants to sketch every day? I was a quick-draw artist who got used to assignments in tricky locations, and to the rush.

Perhaps,
if I'd had more time,
more light,
or just a place to settle in with a stash of colored pencils,
life might have been too cushy
to draw.

Drawing of Chris Giftos by Vail Barrett.

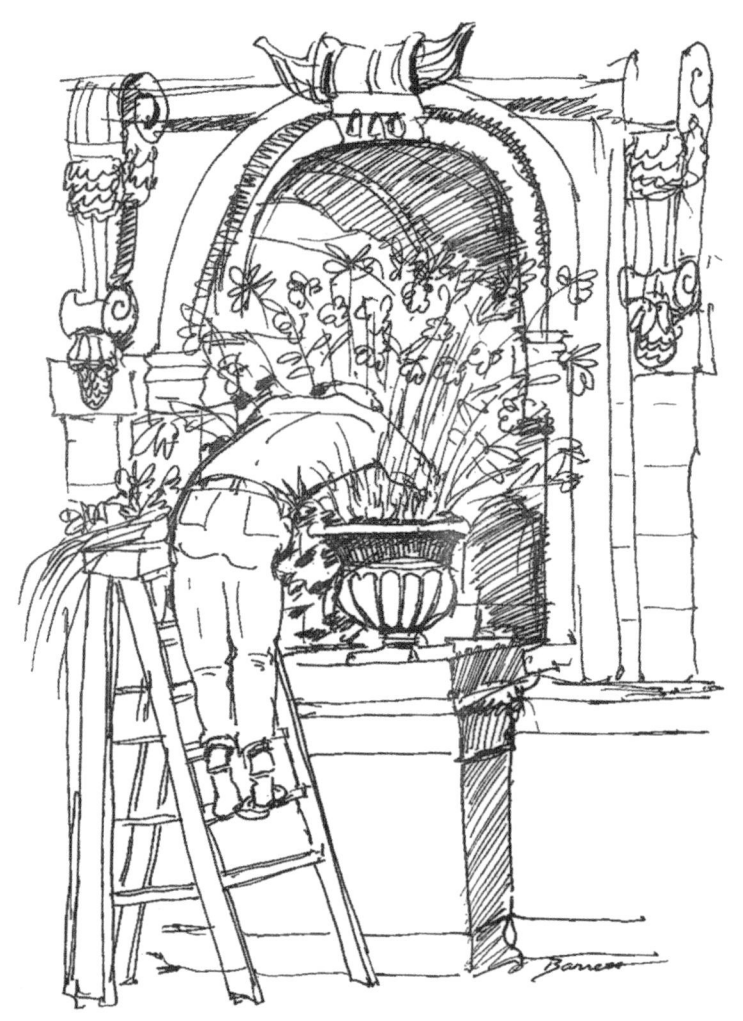

Chapter 2

Chris Giftos, Floral Master

The sky is turning indigo-blue when Chris Giftos goes down to the New York City Flower Market, a stretch of storefronts lining the north and south sides of 28th Street, between 6th and 7th Avenues, but like no other market you've ever seen. From five to seven in the morning, business happens between the chaos of double-parked cars, trucks and vans, yet the police are not handing out tickets because by noon, it'll all be over.

Vendors give Chris a high five and a head's up on what to expect from the Dutch Aalsmeer Flower Auction (the size of 250 football fields) or what's coming in from locals. Dedicated upstate growers and Long Island nurseries provide native specialties. Everything looks dewy fresh and shelf life is a prime consideration.

Over a century ago, Richard Morris Hunt, one of the founding trustees of the Met—as well as the most fashionable architect of his day—designed the classical Fifth Avenue façade and the majestic Great Hall that is the main entrance to the Metropolitan Museum of Art. And for over three decades, Chris Giftos added the iconic welcome of weekly-changing bouquets.

The Met used to be closed to the public on Mondays, but as soon as deliveries arrive, Chris climbs a ten-foot ladder. Assistants have already dismantled the previous week's arrangements in the galvanized tin liners, fabricated according to the master's specifications. Other props are spread out, spatchcock-style, on the floor. It is *mise en place* before the cooking starts. Chris is on autopilot, stripping leaves from stems with his Swiss Army knife. He will repeat this procedure with each bouquet in the four surrounding niches, and the fifth one—the bull's eye—in the crosshairs of the Great Hall, forming a classic quincunx arrangement, the harmonious, five-pointed pattern that appears in art, nature, and computer technologies.

Since ancient times, geometric quincunx groupings have been used in landscape design, often in rows to efficiently guide winds through lines of

An engraved plate from Batty Langley's *New Principles of Gardening* (1728). It shows "A Plantation of Forrest Trees to defend the Fruit from Northern winds" and when looked at diagonally you can see their quincunx arrangement.

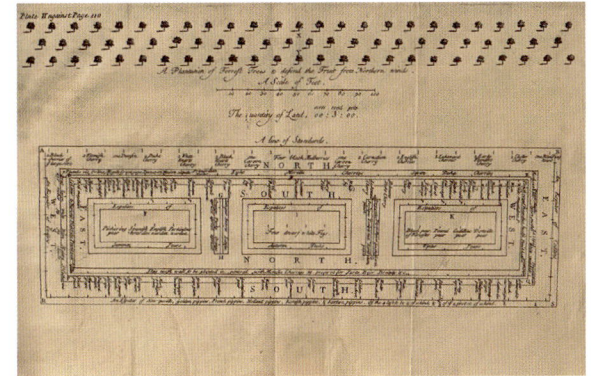

planted trees. But more recently, Thomas Edison had a quincunx tattooed on his right forearm, and, in the hood, a quincunx arrangement can be code for time spent in jail where the outer four dots represent prison walls and the inner one the prisoner.

All urns are filled with identical materials, and though I might ask myself, *Which of these speaks to me today?*, my favorite is predictably the center bouquet with the Renaissance chiaroscuro effect that exaggerates light and dark contrasts. Still, can you imagine how shocked I was, coming in one morning—and for the following two months—when the center arrangement was missing? The guards, always first to know of any hanky-panky, explained that someone high up was not pleased and ordered it removed. An important donation of Tiepolo's 18th-century *The Triumph of Marius* had been installed in coveted real estate at the top of the Grand Stairs and the watercooler talk was that this monumental painting was not to be blocked by flowers.

It took five hours—up and down a ladder—to stage the muscular yet romantic bouquets. And when completed, Chris would walk the Great Hall reviewing his work from every angle, making sure each arrangement was ready. He also took pictures. It was before cell-phone photography and he always sent Polaroids to Met trustee Lila Acheson Wallace, with a written description of the flowers and branches that he used. No one told him to do that. Chris just felt it was the least he owed her.

Mrs. Wallace was an avid gardener and, together with her husband, co-founder of *Reader's Digest*, which was, for a time, thought to be the most widely circulated periodical in the world. My mother kept stacks of *Reader's Digest* and I would read their condensed versions of bestsellers printed on only slightly better paper than pulp magazines.

As a trustee, Mrs. Wallace was also one of the Met's largest single benefactors. She took her philanthropy seriously, and the museum's hospitality personally. She handled the Met like her many homes and wanted visitors to know that they were welcome.

By Thursday morning, the droopers were removed and fresh flowers were added. Again, out came the 10-ft ladder. Again, Chris got up on his perch before the doors opened to the crowds. And when he came down, he walked the Great Hall, making sure his bouquets were ready for their public. Around 40,000 visitors could be expected on a holiday weekend. One rainy, windy, post-Thanksgiving Friday, I heard a guard say they had ticked in 32,000 by 4 p.m. and were doing over 100 coats an hour in the checkroom. Thomas Hoving Jr., the savvy former director, who sought to make the Met a popular institution, said he could always tell how busy it was on the weekends by the buildup of fluffy clumps of dust and debris that collected in every corner.

The first time I met Chris Giftos, he politely—but in no uncertain terms—corrected me regarding his job title.

"Abbie, I am not Director of Flowers. Everyone knows there is only one Director: Philippe de Montebello."

Or "Philly Cheesecake," as the veteran guards nicknamed the long-time aristocratic director of the Met. The gossip of the guards was juicy, everything from who was just fired, to who was working the night shift at the Met Gala. Of course, before volunteering themselves for the Gala, the guards always asked, "Who's coming?", in case it was only riff raff.

But though Chris's title was actually "Manager of Special Events," he really is, more than anything, a "Floral Master."

Chris might tell you that he was in the right place, at the right time and that "I dropped every name I could" to get there, modestly asserting that his success stems from luck: "I was there when the museum was tripling in size, and I grew into the job." Nevertheless, by combining business and art, Chris made the Met a leader in floral installations. He traveled across the country, giving flower demos at luncheons, while encouraging art museums to find their own Mrs. Wallace to underwrite welcoming bouquets—not mere nosegays, but rather something more in line with Mrs. Wallace's unprecedented bequest to the public in perpetuity. Chris said his budget was $2,500 to $3,000 a week wholesale, or about $12,000 retail, in those days. But for Chris Giftos, who was born in Astoria, Queens, studied to become an accountant and in between played a French horn in the army, Mrs. Wallace's support and friendship was an astonishing contribution on a more intimate level. As Chris told me, "Imagine encouraging an artist to do whatever they wanted, giving them carte blanche to create with a no-holds-barred profusion of blooming flowers."

Chris got into the business when he was a teenager, making deliveries and mopping floors at a florist in Queens. From the beginning, he loved working around flowers for the smell alone. He also enjoyed a challenge. During his salad days, long before New York City's recycling law, Chris bragged—*soto voce*—about running the same arrangements from one event to the next, then using the leftovers for funeral wreaths. At 22, this young man's love of flowers was about to triumph over the prospective respectability of becoming a Certified Public Accountant. In 1962, Chris approached Christatos & Koster, the legendary Madison Avenue flower shop run by his fellow Greeks, with a customer base of Astor, Rockefeller, and Paley. It was also where the Met bought their flowers.

I remember Christatos & Koster's enormous windows even if I could not see the lush vegetation through the condensation buildup on the glass. The shop's wide awnings—reminiscent of marquee tents that protected their clients' fashionable gigs from inclement weather at the tony East End of Long Island, one of the country's most expensive ZIP codes—shielded delicate inventory from the sun's rays at the southeast corner of 63rd Street. Matrons, who had a staff of maids and liveried chauffeurs, shopped with standing orders and house accounts. No cash was passed. It was before local Korean delis sold cut flowers next to the salad bar, and a bit intimidating if all you wanted were a few daisies for a bedside glass of water. Yet Christatos & Koster thrived in a carriage-trade era when Madison Avenue was still a two-way street, not lined with flagship boutiques but idiosyncratic enterprises where you could catch Jolie Gabor, mother of Magda, Eva, and Zsa Zsa, hawking costume jewelry. Or just imagine a shop that only sold handmade lace, or a store with little oak chairs and children's books in the front, quirky vintage volumes in the back. That was where I got my first "first-edition," a cloth-covered jacketless book entitled *Embroidered Cross-Stitched Samplers* with tipped-in colored plates that gave me ideas for the cover of *The Potted Herb*. Those were the days when you could still see stately Mr. William Greenberg Jr. decorating delicate wedding cakes in the window, even when the city's swankiest butchers lowered their Venetian blinds and closed for lunch. And speaking of lunch, Schrafft's at 78th Street was where the Upper East Side went slumming if they were not at the Colony Club, the fabled gilt-edged gathering place for the social elite and international jet set—equally noted for banning miniskirts. At least the Colony provided a private room with satin pillows and tidy meals on silver trays for patrons' doggies. But, more significantly, like most of these service enterprises along the Avenue, they extended credit when loyal regulars were down on their luck.

Chris tells me his first customer was Greta Garbo, and I believe him. But he didn't know who she was, and I believe that too. When I cut cheese in a

Drawn from my living room windows,
this is the Carlyle Hotel, with its looming
presence over Upper East Side.

Chris Giftos, Floral Master

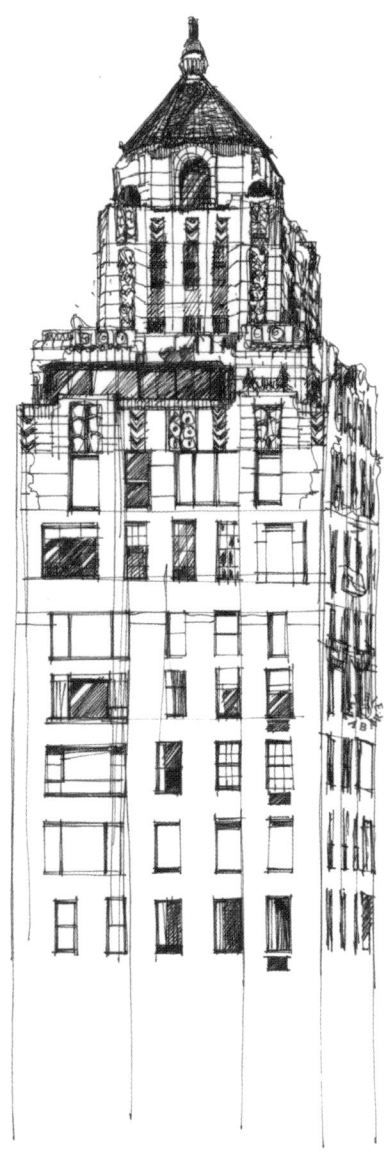

gourmet food store up the Avenue, it was a standing joke that I recognized nobody. But as soon as Warren Beatty came in and asked for a large ripe round of a gooey Brie—along with his usual two-dozen oranges—I knew enough to suggest that I run his delivery... after I took off the shame of a dirty apron. If you didn't smell or look like trouble, a white-gloved attendant would personally take you up in the Carlyle's passenger elevator to a guest's suite to earn the tip. But for the record, a towel-clad Warren Beatty stuck out his naked arm and grabbed the grub. I collected myself, turned around and remembered the elevator. It was there to take me back down.

Shortly after the Greta Garbo walk-in, the Met ordered 100 centerpieces. Chris also overheard that the museum was looking for an Assistant Banquet Manager. Christatos & Koster, like any of those service shops, doubled as a hothouse for neighborhood gossip. So, that was when, in 1970, the young man from Queens who loved the scent of flowers and was 10 years old when he first visited the Met, finally made his move. Chris Giftos suggested to the Metropolitan Museum of Art that they need their own floral designer. And they should hire him. Full time.

Even though it meant a cut in pay, Chris Giftos became the Met's first Floral Designer, as well as Assistant Banquet Manager. He reckoned that with a father who called himself a "chef," but really was a short-order cook, he could handle food. No matter that banquets, galas, and catering turned out to be a whole other cow—as Chris says: "I got on-the-job training. I learned to put a fork on the left."

Besides, Chris was a natural charmer. The ladies loved him. One of his biggest fans was New York society doyenne Pat Buckley, wife of the conservative intellectual writer William F. Buckley Jr. She was a prominent fund-raiser and served as chairwoman of the Costume Institute Gala for 17 years (yes, there was life before Anna Wintour). "I relied on Chris heavily," Pat said. "He's got an extraordinary feel for anything that grows and is the nicest man I know."

It's no wonder that Chris Giftos was chosen to escort Princess Di around the galleries. Besides, who else could tactfully tell Emily Rafferty, the first woman president of the Met, when she was sitting up on the auditorium stage with a skirt above her knees, "We see London, we see France..."?

But he also oversaw hundreds of yearly events, from cocktail parties to elaborate corporate dinners. As well as attending to every detail from the invitations, the route that guests would walk through the museum, to the decor, food, wine, and entertainment. He was a down-to-earth guy whose greatest concerns reflected those of any party-giver. "I had to make sure the flowers survived the event, the sound system worked, and the entrées came out hot."

In 2003, after 33 years, the Met threw their farewell reception for Chris in the Temple of Dendur—a gift from Egypt to the USA, that was actually reconstructed in the Met and became one of the museum's most popular attractions—where the flowers for the two-million-dollar Nouvelle Society Tisch–Steinberg wedding were his doing. Emily Rafferty asked me to donate one of my drawings as a gift to Chris on behalf of the Met. I was shocked. Nevertheless, I chose the one with forced forsythia branches because they were his favorite arrangements, and at six in the evening, I walked behind Chris's little nieces, who were following his most honored guests—an Archbishop and six humble Greek priests from Astoria, in long black robes, who were full of pride for their native son.

I did my first drawing of a bouquet in the Great Hall while sitting on the floor, lower back against the wall. It was Saturday the 13th of August, 1994. The museum had been open for half an hour; the place was packed. I carried the stool that I did not have yesterday. Three guards had already approached me. I told them, "See? I have the stool now and I will be gone by 10:30. Please." One guard told me to put on my shoes.

Prospects improved the following day, thanks to a young guard, about my age. In addition to her regular assignment, Marissa was keeping an eye on my drawing and whispered she loved what I was doing, every time I added another stroke. But, unfortunately for me, the summer blooms remained too tightly closed.

To catch the exuberance of monumental flowers, on a scale no larger than my hand, in a fleeting moment when they were exhaling—that was the challenge that drew me in. My drawings were not fine botanical studies on vellum. I couldn't do that, even if I tried. I took artistic license. Luckily, I also took notes. But there had to be a better way.

I finally called the Office of Special Events on 4 October and left a nervous voicemail message:
"Hello, my name is Abbie Zabar and I want to please draw the bouquets in the Great Hall. Before the museum opens. Is that possible?"
"I know you. You're the artist," Chris said when he called me back. In retrospect, he told me that he didn't think I understood what a compliment this was. At the suggestion of my Upper East Side gallery, BlumHelman, I had donated one of my paper collages, the size of a postage stamp, to the 1979 Lenox Hill Neighborhood House Gala. It was of a Nantucket dirt road. Chris had the winning bid.

And if that isn't coincidental enough, I later learned that several of my long, multi-paneled landscape collages of the New Croton Reservoir were purchased for the *Reader's Digest* Collection after their curator saw them at the Cooper-Hewitt Museum's 1985 *Cut-Paper* exhibit. "Right time, right place," as Chris might have said. The corporate headquarters for *Reader's Digest* used to be a stone's throw from that reservoir.

A bouquet as displayed in its niche
in the Great Hall at the Met Museum.

Chris Giftos, Floral Master

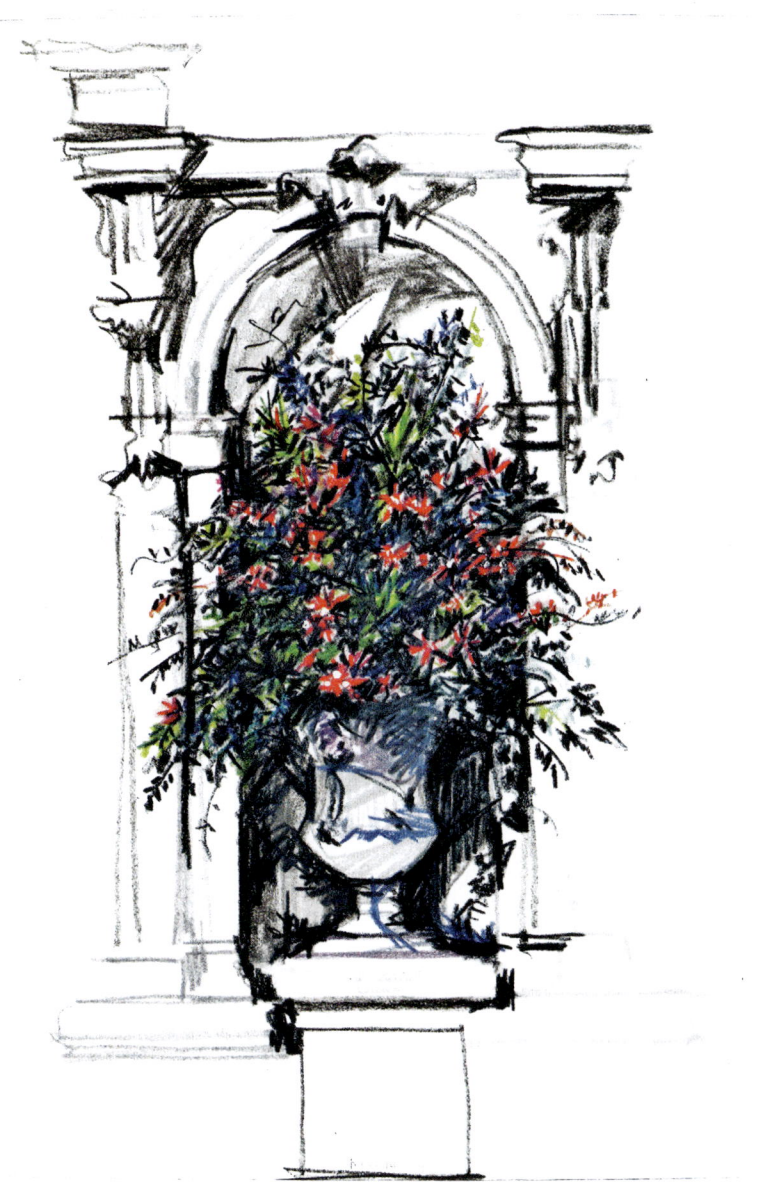

Small glass of water with a few oxeye daisies, drawn on the backside of an envelope.

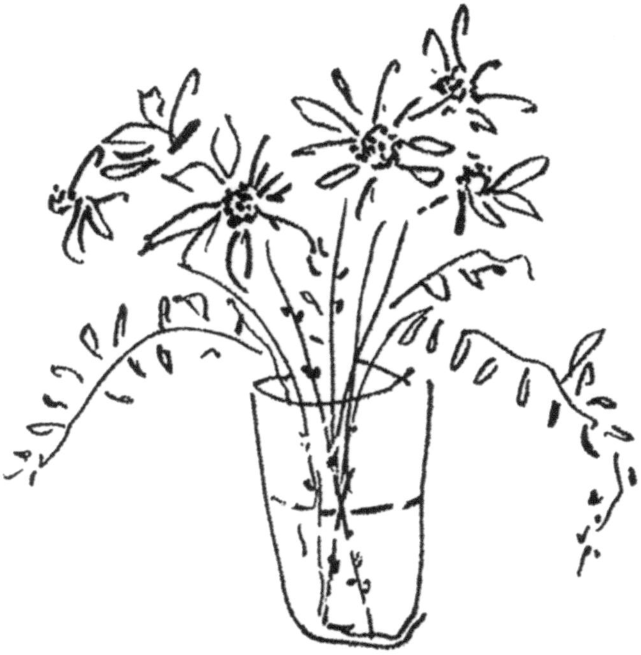

Chapter 3
The Constance Spry School of Flower Arranging

I t is early morning, and little green lorries are dropping off massive bundles of flora on a cobbled backstreet that could be an engraving straight from the pages of a Charles Dickens classic.

We were still married when my husband signed us up for a week of cooking classes at 31 Marylebone Lane—London's Le Cordon Bleu and the brainchild of chef Dione Lucas and Rosemary Hume, a food authority, writer, and accomplished cook. But after sitting there until noon, I finally got up and walked to number 98, which bore the intriguing shingle: "The Constance Spry School of Flower Arranging."

In 1946, Hume and Spry opened Winkfield Place in Berkshire, a finishing school where well-bred young women were taught domestic arts, rather than how to walk in high heels. The setting was a large white country house on the edge of a forest with spacious gardens where Spry, the consummate rosarian, cultivated her antique roses. Students learned to compose bouquets with brambles from her woods, as well as how to prepare everything from crown roasts to meringues, or simply serve a breakfast that was fresh, hot, and easy. There were daily classes in secretarial work and dressmaking practicalities such as sewing on a button and the proper way to wash, iron, and fold laundry— or, for that matter, clean everything from bathtubs to crystal chandeliers. Hume and Spry were zoning in on the solar plexus of British country life: how to engineer a beautiful and gracious home, pre-Martha Stewart.

Constance Spry believed that *every* household—even the humblest— is destined to be a thing of beauty. Which reminds me of when I served scrambled eggs on glossy green galax leaves, for a lack of clean plates. "You are one of the best *maîtresses de maison* in America," said Hubert de Givenchy about my cockamamie-boho style. I had met the Parisian couturier while cutting cheese and now we were sitting on the back deck of a Nantucket Island beach shack with weathered gray shingles in a setting that he loved because it was *"très sauvage."*

Constance Spry's books have been published in hard cover throughout the world, but it is a dog-eared wisp of a paperback—bought at her school—that remains my favorite. Maybe because of the provenance. Or perhaps it's because *How to do the Flowers* (1953) was speaking to folks like me with no frou-frou flower experience. At the age of 43, Constance showed the public that there is beauty in brown twigs. She used everything from roadside weeds to leftover withered pods. From lichen-covered logs, previously never given a second thought, to hawthorn limbs, newly liberated from hedgerows along with their shriveled-up fruit, although mockingbirds in my rooftop garden avoid those desiccated, burgundy-colored berries like the plague. She always started her arrangements with selections from the compost heap, gathering crispy dried leaves past their prime, and knowing that insect-chewed foliage made everything better.

By honoring the local, familiar and commonplace while using formerly snubbed gifts of nature, Constance Spry's arrangements were nothing short of showstoppers. She made you look at pastures, farmland, and wildlife up-close and personal. She broke down barriers, believing that the joy of working with flowers is at everyone's fingertips, while remaining true to her mission, flagrantly defiant of Victorian and Edwardian ideas of floral beauty. She raided attics for makeshift vessels. Anything capable of holding water "could have been a contender" (forgive me, Marlon Brando). The "found aesthetic" worked for her and always will for me. Unapologetically banal as they are, run-of-the-mill Ball canning jars remain my go-to.

If flower arranging is an analogy for democracy, then our gal Connie was a social reformer. Her humility was her genius.

That's not to say Constance Spry would never use a silver vase to hold asparagus ferns. She also writes, in another of her dog-eared books on my shelf, *Flowers in House and Garden* (1937), "I think a single rose in a clear glass, the stem showing, the thorns outlined with tiny bubbles is exquisite."

A week of two-hour private sessions at the Constance Spry School of Flower Arranging were my favorite tutorials, ever. No wonder I kept the notes. How compelling to learn something altogether new, to feel what it's like to be a child again. After sitting in a Cordon Bleu kitchen classroom, I knew where I belonged.

I worked with the same Constance Spry tutor every morning, but with a different container daily and new cut stems. We began with chitchat about unfamiliar flowers and their Latin names, which I found impossible to pronounce. As she built up the scaffolds of her arrangements, mostly there was talk about principles. I could hardly wait to start. I've always been less about theory and more enthusiastic about hands-on activities. I can watch a plumber install copper-pipe fittings for hours and never get bored.

Our prep table was waist-high. Clippings fell to the floor. We were standing in a puddle of greens. Sketchpad on my right, I was drawing, taking notes, and watching as best I could. It reminded me of when I worked for a newspaper, drawing from life onsite. And now, drawing while arranging flowers. As fast as I could.

It brought back memories of weekends when I slept at grandma's. She was the only one in the family with a television. Jon Gnagy's Saturday *Learn to Draw* programs were my entertainment. He swore that if you just got a grip on a ball, a cone, a cube, and a cylinder, you could draw anything. When my TV artist guru built up his winter landscapes, using the side of a kneaded eraser to create snow in a forest, I was spellbound. His time slot was 15 minutes. In a frantic attempt to keep up with what he was doing, I Scotch-taped tissue paper to the TV screen and traced whatever he did. By the time the familiar little jingle came on, Jon Gnagy had hung the frame around his artwork. Showtime was over. My week at Constance Spry flew by just as fast.

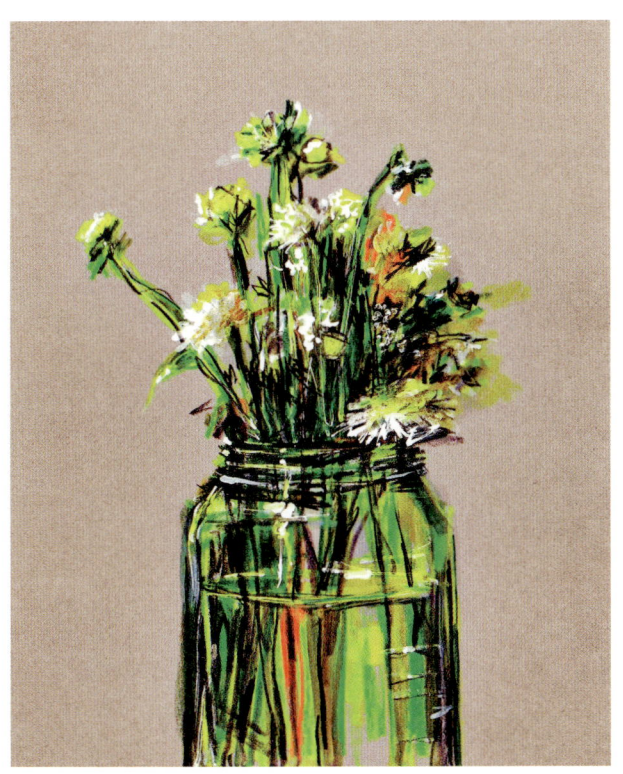 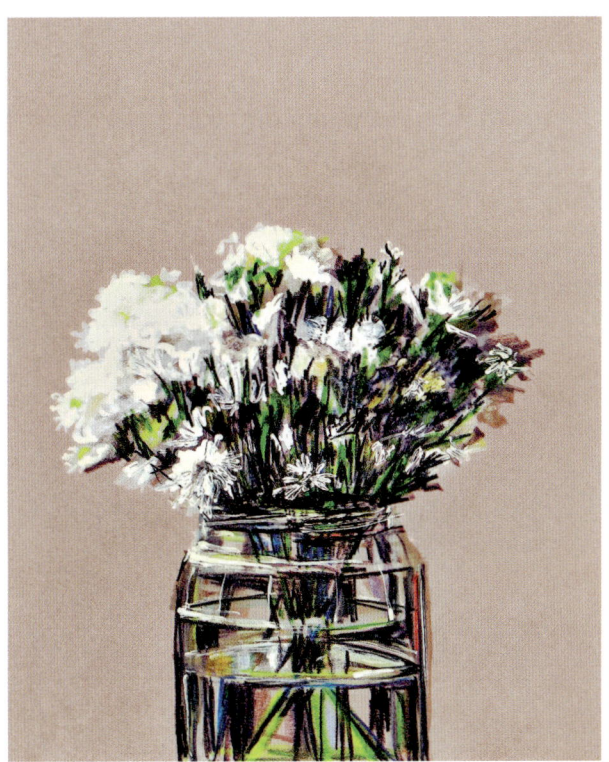

Left: Shriveling dahlias in a glass jar.
Right: Little white mums in a glass jar.

Bouquet

For my fifth and final morning, I was allowed into the Vase Room, nothing more than a well-lit, white-lacquered corridor. After days of trying to mimic what I was being shown, suddenly I could select a vessel that spoke to me. It was my mortarboard moment. I reached for a woven-willow bicycle basket. "Unusual choice," said the tutor, loud enough to make me feel like I'd screwed up already.

My arrangement was equally odd. And extremely horizontal. Branches shot crossways like out-of-control hair cowlicks. Wild-and-wooly hazel catkins and flowers with tongue-twister names were slanting left and right. I did not know a ranuncula from a multi-petaled cabbage rose, but I was releasing my inner Constance Spry. I was having a ball and, honestly, I really didn't give a hoot. In fact, I felt a raffish sense of freedom, which at that moment in time had been absent for years.

Still, on that final morning—with her back to me and in a clipped British accent—the tutor whispered to my husband when he came to pick me up, "Your wife has a real flair for this."

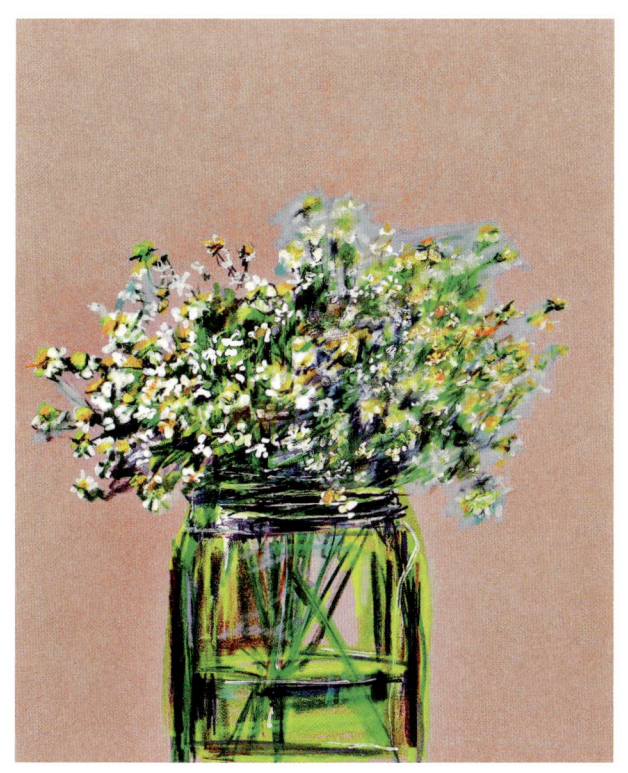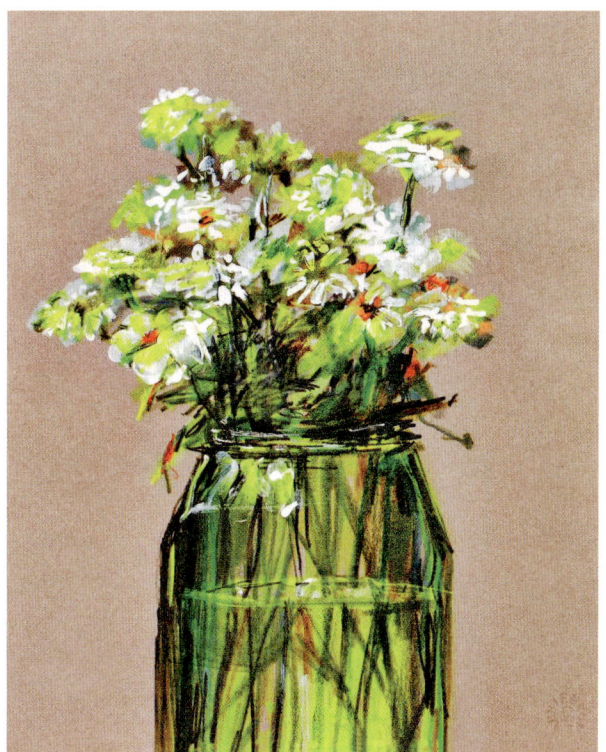

Left: Feverfew in a green glass jar.
Right: Zinnias in a green glass jar.

Jasper Johns' bank.

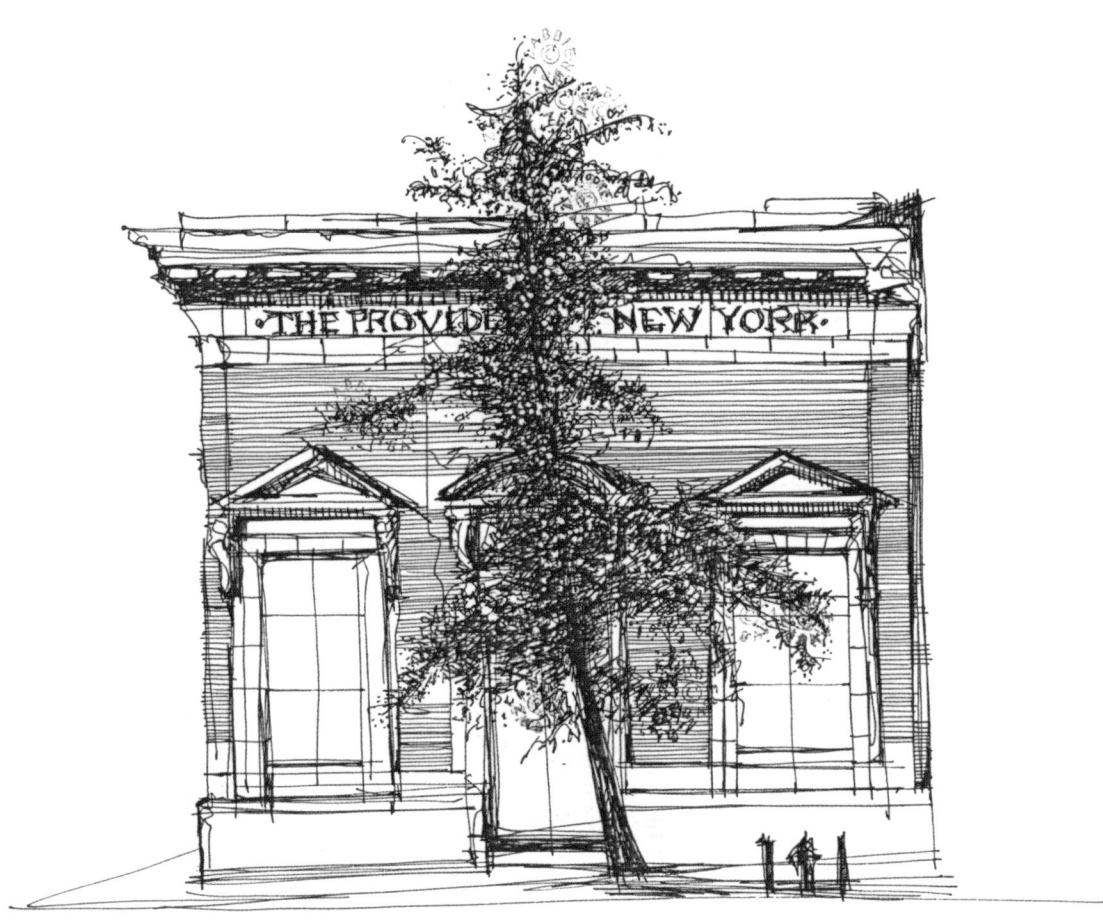

Chapter 4
Struggling Artist Meets Jasper Johns

One miserably hot summer afternoon—sometime before the central air conditioning had been installed—I heard that a drawing was needed to fill out a small Jasper Johns story. The layout department was in a rush; anyone with authority was on a long lunch. *Women's Wear Daily* had a 5 p.m. deadline for all art. I was the most recent hire in a pool of 30 staff artists, give or take a few, depending upon when an infusion of raw talent was needed. I was 20 years old. I drew any assignment tossed on my desk. Or what none of the prima donnas would touch.

The Jasper Johns story was the only one I ever asked for.

I drew for *Home Furnishings Daily*, a Fairchild publication that lived in the shadow of its famous sibling. *Women's Wear Daily* was bitchy and trendy but more solid on business news than *The New York Times*. Yet it was not long before John Fairchild turned *WWD* into the bible of the industry, while single-handedly catapulting or extinguishing careers. And once typesetting started using a bold-face hierarchy in print to describe designers or movie stars, the trade daily became the holy writ of the social world as well. A similar pecking order filtered down to the editorial and art departments. In other words, the artist who did the cover art was called Page-One Artist, and it was always a "he." *He* was the only artist who could tell an editor what *he* did and did not want to draw. I didn't say "boo." But because I drew fast—no roughs, no comps, no preliminary sketches—they would give me more and more to draw, including an awful lot of subjects that no one who called herself an artist would ever admit to drawing Monday to Friday.

In pen and ink, I did everything from electric can openers to toaster ovens with new-fangled buttons, the same chrome objects that Roy Lichtenstein was painting with zigzag reflections and the blown-up Ben Day dots of newsprint comic strips. But I can honestly remember feeling relieved they were not throwing me Page-One art, like sofas fresh out of High Point with recent 17th-century cabriole legs or newly upholstered wing chairs, because how many ways can you make chintz read like headline news?

Then, as soon as a retailer opened a flagship store, or another boutique moved uptown, *Women's Wear Daily* sent me. Fashion artists don't do architecture. And that was something I could really get off on in pen and ink.

So, it came to pass on an excruciatingly hot afternoon, with empty offices and *Women's Wear Daily* on a rush deadline, that a new guy in the production department—probably with about as much clout as I had—agreed to give me the Jasper Johns assignment.

The air-conditioned car service was waiting to take us down Second Avenue. Fashion editors had perks. I was nervous and excited and tried to explain just who Jasper Johns was. The editor assigned to write the story was always so chic I was scared to death to talk to her. Right then she was bored and wilted, with half-moon sweat stains on her Jacki-O sheath. I thought Jasper Johns deserved better.

I also thought, I should write the story. Had I ever written anything before? No, but at least I'd bring enthusiasm. I stared out the window and wished I were going by myself. The subway would have been fine, but the driver took us to Essex Street where it crosses Houston. Sitting on the corner was a proper piece of Palladian architecture that used to house a savings and loan operation, back when banks conveyed confidence through classic façades. Now it was home to Jasper Johns. The limestone edifice was a monument to the artist's success, and a symbol of the money being spent on contemporary art. But why shouldn't America's highest-paid living artist own a bank? Jasper Johns followed on the heels of second-generation abstract expressionism, and these days his work was being cherry-picked by a cadre of new collectors responding to the easy images of pop art—

folks who owned taxicab companies and prided themselves on knowing the existential meaning of a Campbell's soup can.

In a few hours, the Merce Cunningham Dance Company would be giving a benefit performance of John Cage's music in Jasper's bank. Art "happenings" didn't get more bold-faced than that. Nor sweeter smelling— it had the scent of a social scene. Yet this was before phones took the photos and, because there would be a delay of a day or more until *Women's Wear Daily* published the black-and-white headshots of the guests—plus a few artists if they were famous enough—for the time being, the production department needed a line-drawing of Jasper's bank as filler in tomorrow's paper. The layout was planned for a slot that was one column wide by two inches deep. It didn't matter that the goddamn building took up the whole corner of a city block. Or that a leaning gingko tree was smack in front of the huge entry doors. Another reason drawing from life is tempting. It's unedited.

Jasper Johns is showing me through a space of infinite former grandeur, high as it is wide. Except for a brightly colored sculpture with dented-chrome fenders and rusted car parts, all that's in this empty cube of monumental proportions is voluptuous natural light. I watch two assistants moving the John Chamberlain piece back and forth, but I'm thinking, *Where's all the other art I was hoping to see?* Yet, it crosses my mind how cool it would be if they'd leave the collision smack in the middle for tonight, as if it had actually happened for the Happening.

We are walking from the majestic, voluminous space with bare windows framed in the same dark wood as the coffered ceiling to a back area where a low-hung, acoustic-tile ceiling suggests suburban basements. This space feels like an afterthought, as though someone had said, "How's about a cozy place to curl up in, once everybody's blown away by the big room?" I'm looking at a narrow bed—the kind I sleep in, the kind monks have always slept in. It's barely off the floor and covered with an impressive Navajo blanket because the chief owns the bank. Right next to it, on a table as low as the bed, there are neatly stacked books and a gooseneck lamp with a weighted base, which is throwing off a yellow cast in deep contrast to the natural white light of the big empty space. That's when I catch the small bronze plaque, exactly like the one I saw years ago in a Marcel Duchamp retrospective at the Tate, the first time I went to London. Even then, the vulva in bronze bas-relief was more elegant than erotic. Light is modulating the noble material enough to imbue the casting with religious dignity befitting a bedside crucifix. The subject matter had been deified, the same way Jasper Johns elegantly canonizes a pair of Ballantine Ale cans.

We return to the big empty space where the colossal windows now frame a colorless smoggy sky. Thin red string identifies towers of cookie boxes, just delivered from William Greenberg Desserts.

I start wondering what the hell ever made me ask for this assignment. I'm not feeling good about drawing in Jasper Johns' space. After all, here is the preeminent and leading contender for Most-Important-Artist-of-the-Late-20th-Century. A "Living Legend," as *The New York Times* called him at the time of his 2008 *Gray* show at the Metropolitan Museum of Art. Though he seems indifferent about why I'm here, Jasper Johns is a Southern gentleman, extremely gracious and hospitable. Even paternal, I'd say, as I'm trying to get comfortable in a no-nonsense heavy oak chair like the office furniture from the '40s. Without getting up from where I'm sitting, my eyes are taking crib notes, looking around for what to draw first. I like to start with something easy, counting on the hard stuff falling into place later, the way life usually works.

At least I'm using familiar materials, unforgiving as they are. I've got my favorite pen and a brand-new, black, leatherette-bound sketchbook with sewn-in pages, which aren't meant to be torn out like I do with spiral pads as soon as I make a mistake. I shake up the Rapidograph, even though the instructions say that's a no-no. I need to hear the tinsel-thin steel thread moving freely in the nib. I rub my wrist across the fresh sheet of clean white paper as if I'm stroking the back fur of a dog that I'm not so sure about, but I want us to be friends anyway. I've repeated this overture to a drawing I don't know how many times before.

I feel nervous. I feel excited. More nervous than excited. I feel the new guy in production should be fired.

Jasper Johns goes over to the island kitchen counter and starts unwrapping cookie boxes meant for tonight. He lets the red strings fall to the floor as if he were untying a silk bathrobe from Charvet on the Place Vendôme, a retrieval job for those who dream of being a sous-chef to a living legend.

The chef de cuisine is standing behind an orderly lineup of liquor bottles and says he's going to fix me something special.

In no time, Jasper Johns comes over with a plate of cookies and a pink drink with bubbles. Not what he's having. It's embarrassing. *Do I really look that young?* I wonder. Then, just like that, the living legend sits down across from me at the big round oak table. He's knocking back his drink and mentions my drawing directly with pen to paper. "No roughs, no comps, no preliminary sketches," I mutter to myself.

My heart is pumping. I can hardly catch my breath. All I'm thinking is, *Is Jasper Johns impressed?* My pen starts tracing what I've already drawn, contour lines meant to be left alone.

I've stopped looking at what I should be seeing.

An ancient lion sculpture on the way to the Temple of Dendur at the Met Museum.

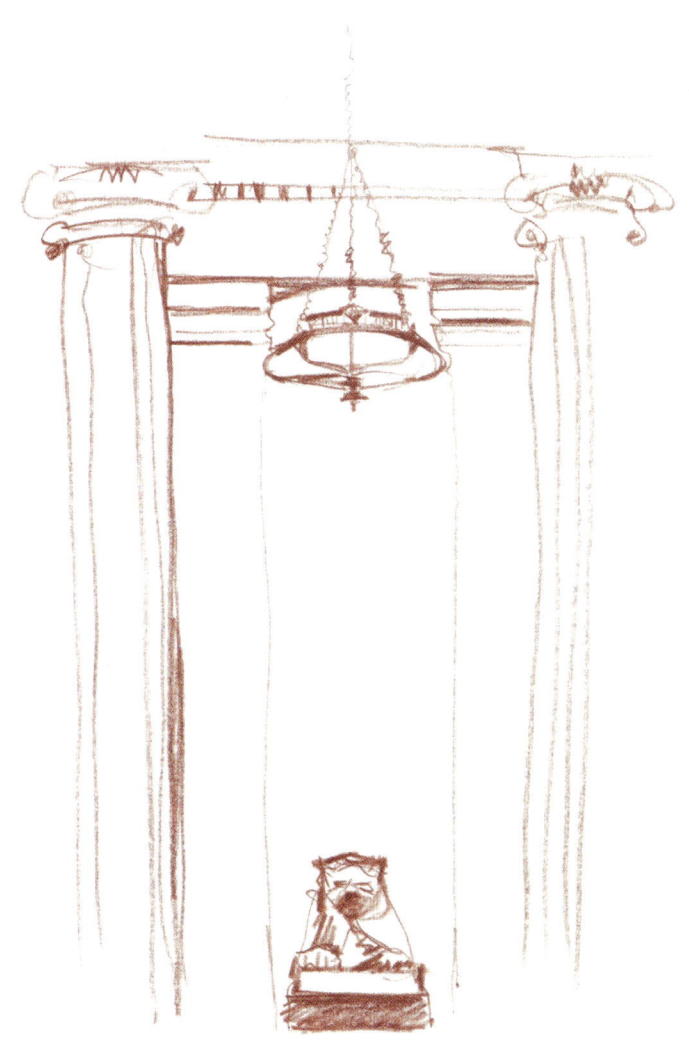

A bouquet in situ for Thanksgiving weekend.

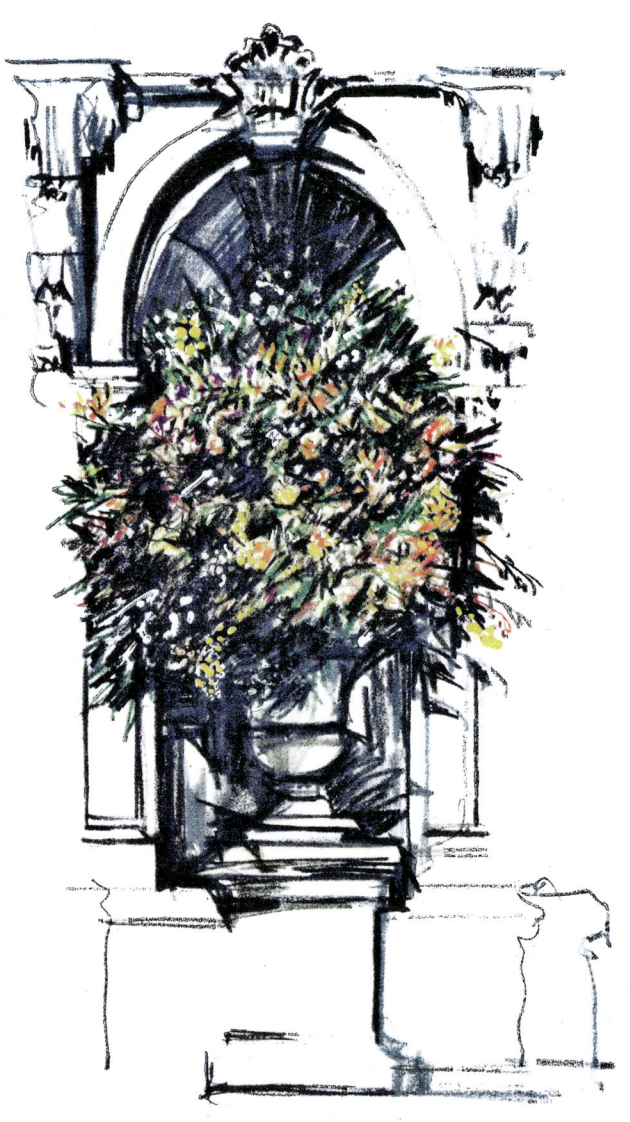

Chapter 5

Mother, Me, and the Met

Bouquet

I t was early morning when the call came from the city morgue.

The young woman went down to identify the blond-haired man who had collapsed in a well-fitted suit on a sidewalk in midtown Manhattan. He was a custom tailor, after all.

She would then return to their tidy one-bedroom Upper West Side apartment where relatives were already gathering. And I was hopping around like an Easter rabbit with a sympathy basket on my head. Aunts and uncles thought it was a disgrace. "Can't someone stop her?" several of them said. But on that day in May 1949, I was not yet four years old and if it is any consolation to my critics, I still wear a scar in the middle of my forehead, years after I fell down with a picot-edged basket on my head the day my daddy died.

I did not come from a literary family. Nor a garden-making dynasty. Nor was I the farmer's daughter. I didn't know the difference between soil and dirt. I did not speak botanical Latin. There wasn't a single volume on natural history in my home when I was growing up. Not even a back-pocket guide to local birds, no matter that mine were only pigeons. But what goes missing often etches deeply into our soul. We had one lonely little jade plant on a windowsill. It came from the basement of the local Woolworth's store, where it had been growing under fluorescent lights alongside caged canaries and forgiving fish. Even though *The Potted Herb*—the first book I ever wrote—became a gardening classic, to this day, I am nothing more than a self-taught gardener.

To support the two of us, my mother worked in the garment district where she announced, to anyone within earshot, that her daughter has a God-given talent. But she never said anything of the sort to me. The young widow became single-minded about getting her only child into drawing classes and art schools on a bookkeeper's salary. Applications piled up on top of the editions of *Reader's Digest*, as did my guilt for not completing home-test entrance exams. Still, her love and due diligence paid off.

After graduating from Music & Art, artistic crown jewel of five, free, specialized New York City public high schools (famous for uber-talented beatniks and Joan Baez look-a-likes), I began commuting to Brooklyn, where DeKalb Avenue walk-ups were buttressed by turn-of-the-century corner mansions for parvenues. And it was one such nouveau tycoon, Charles Pratt, whose eponymous college I attended on a scholarship. Yet, it crossed my mind, *If they liked my drawings so much, why was I now being taught how to draw?*

But Vincent Lazaro's classes were the most eye-opening in four years at Pratt Institute. There would be no yellow-tracing-paper overlays, no false starts, no roughs, no comps, no preliminary sketches. "And no more pencils, no more erasers, only pen and ink", he said. And then he laid it on the line, "No more looking down at your paper, draw what you see, not what you remember."

At the end of his introduction, I made a beeline to one of two art stores en route to catching the subway back to Queens, where I was now living with my mother after she remarried. Both Jake's and Charlie's had a solidarity of followers, harsh fluorescent lights, and open shelves with art supplies for every discipline, from architectural scale rulers to blocks of modeling clay. I walked the aisles, collecting drawing pads of different sizes and assorted brands of India ink (but no erasers) and then I went—the long way around—to an enormous checkout counter that handled the most unwieldly art boards I had ever seen. After all the stalling, I finally asked for my first Rapidograph, the Mercedes of technical-drawing pens, usually kept behind locked glass doors. Shortly, I would master cleaning the German precision instruments, with their tinsel-thin steel nibs that notoriously clogged at inconvenient moments.

In 1966, I graduated with a Bachelor of Fine Arts degree and a white-knuckle way of drawing. I then had to figure out if I would be an artist or a designer. "Sweetheart, you'd make a living," my mother kept reminding me about the latter. But then I met Elaine Lustig Cohen, the artist who was also a graphic and interior designer, who recommended my work to her friend Massimo Vignelli. I might have worshipped contemporary Italian design, but I'd never previously heard of this designer, who coined the phrase, "If you can design one thing, you can design anything." Isn't that right on?

At our first meeting, Massimo, one of the hottest-looking graphic designers of the 20th century, handed me some glossy aerial photographs that were as black-and-white as his hip offices, the New York City headquarters of Unimark International—another name that drew a blank. They needed a freehand, pen-and-ink, bird's-eye perspective of an upstate urban-renewal project. It was my first freelance job, due back in a week. I liked the challenge and saw no reason to ask for an extended deadline.

Massimo would like my oversized drawing, especially all the nitty-gritty rooftops that I really got off on, but *not* my bill. Then, with the most charming Italian accent, he added, "*Cara mia* Abbie, you need to be *professionale* about what you charge." I honestly do not remember how much *more* I was paid. Still, I'll never forget Massimo announcing that he'd be calling. But in one of those fork-in-the-road scenarios, I had been offered a fulltime job as a staff artist at *Home Furnishings Daily*, a trade publication with 5 p.m. deadlines, where I had interviewed a couple of weeks before. Getting paid to draw Monday to Friday… *I* would have paid *them*.

I have always loved a good museum gift and book store. I consider it the pre-game show. And in the Met's retail space, which kept annexing coveted real estate, I had hot-rodded all the remarkable collections in their world-famous upstairs galleries by studying the postcards first.

In the late 1940s, the museum revealed plans for a new restaurant that would be housed in the Lamont Wing's Roman courtyard, to be completed in late 1953. Dorothy Draper & Co., considered by some the most influential American interior decorator of the past century, was to be the designer. They were replacing the old Pompeian courtyard with a pool. *The Fountain of the Muses*, a bronze work commissioned from the Swedish-born sculptor Carl Milles, was slated to be the centerpiece. It is now in Brookgreen Gardens, the sculpture garden and wildlife preserve where I

Bouquet

had been invited to speak in Murrells Inlet in South Carolina, of all places, about my New York City rooftop garden, of all things.

On the weekends, we could take the 79th-Street bus across the park from Riverside Drive, get off at Fifth Avenue, then walk north to the Met. But first, we went to lunch, upscale from my favorite, Horn & Hardart, but still nothing more than a canteen where they might have redone the setting but not the menu.

My father was 39 and my mother 24 when they married. He used to tell her he hoped they would have a little girl so that she would always have a best friend.

I adored going to art museums with my mother. I don't know when I noticed the flowers, but I loved watching her pour coffee from those nifty little "hottles"—the height of sophistication in such a time-capsule atmosphere.

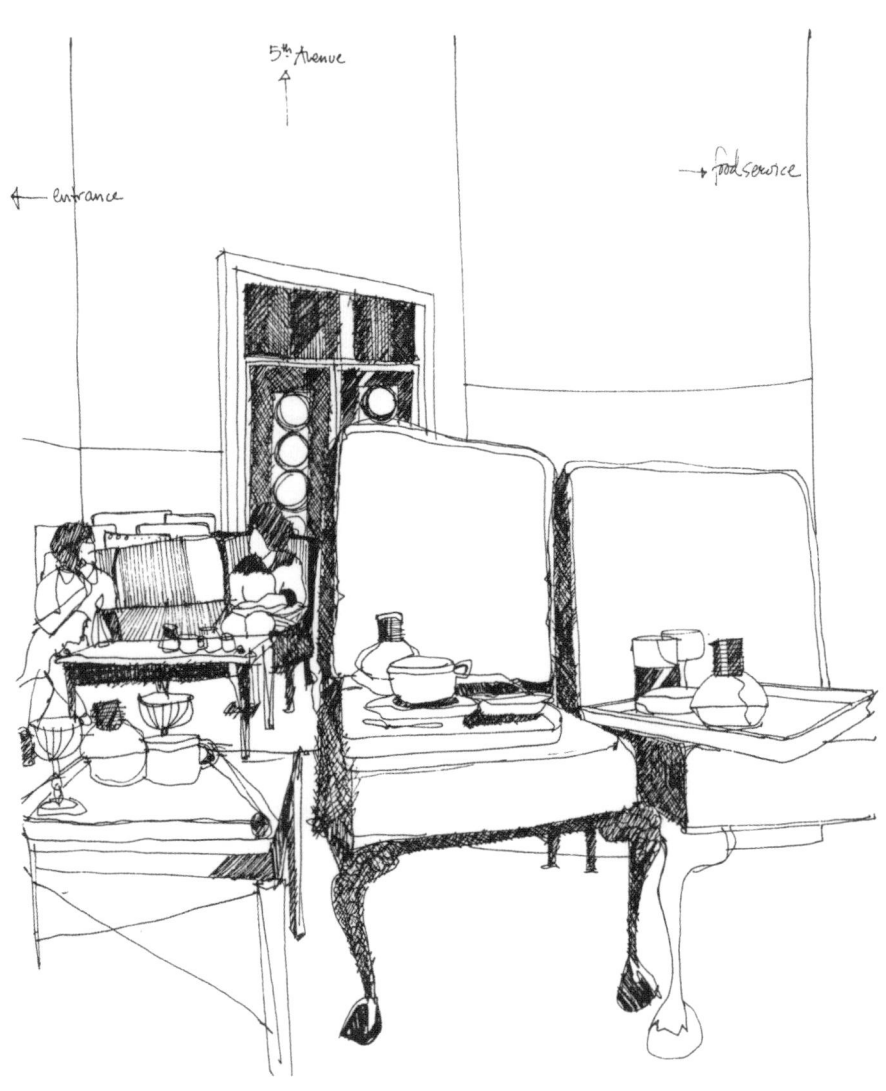

Spring

I n Spring, the grand bouquets held huge palm fronds and variegated large leaves. There were red-hot pokers and the droopy lobster claws of heliconia, also known as false birds of paradise.

4 March:

Just cherry blossoms. Possibly *Prunus* 'Kanzan', one of the most ornamental flowering cherries, because it produces an amazing profusion of rich double-pink flowers held in pendant clusters.

Colored pencil on white paper, 9½ x 9⅞ in

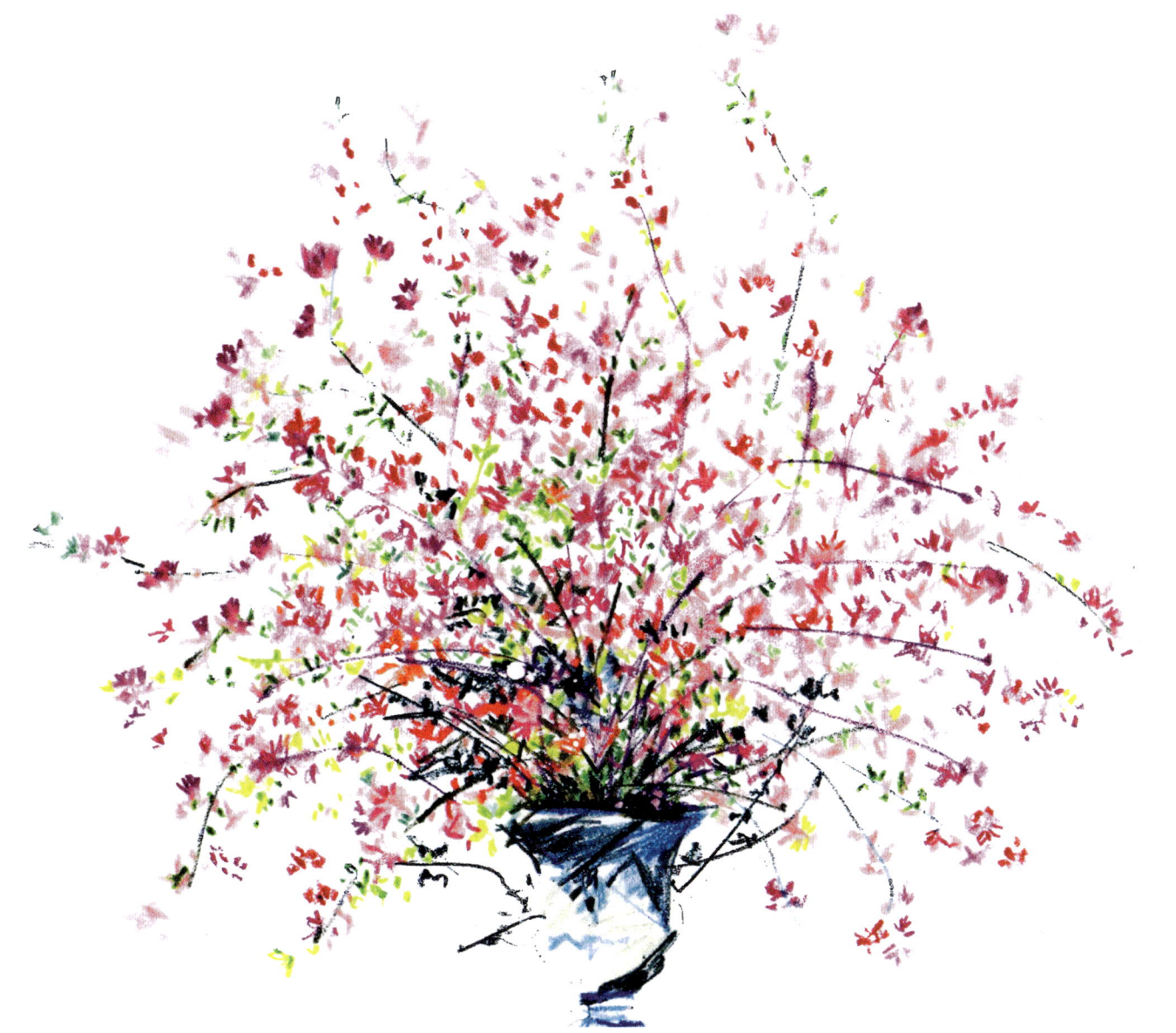

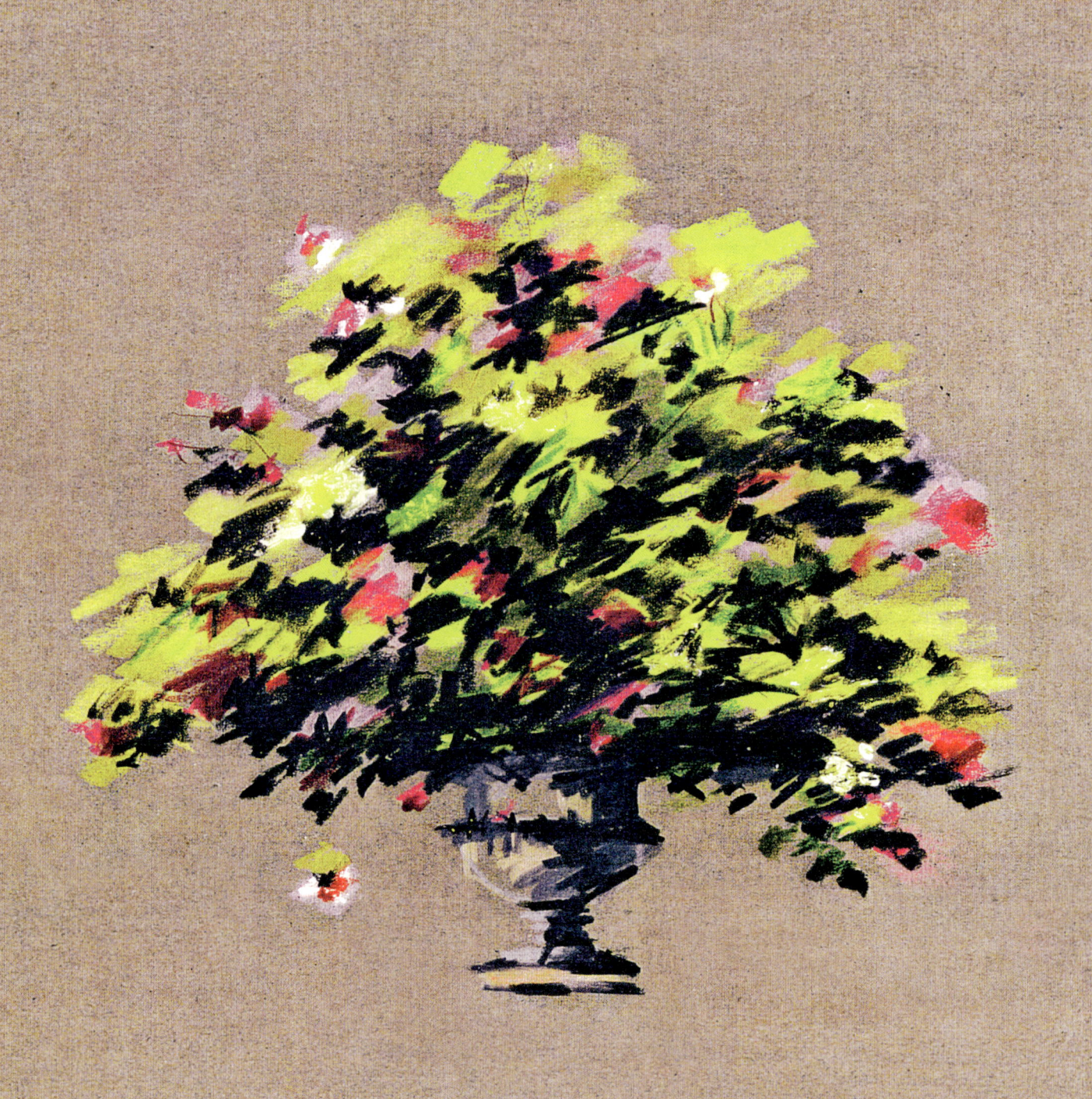

4 March:

Lilies, green and yellow leaves, big red emperor tulips, sprays of cherry blossoms and evergreen leaves.

Colored pencil and smudged whiteout on cardboard with yellow enamel, 8⅞ x 9¼ in

8 March:

Droopy dark red things, cherry blossom branches, palm leaves, canna leaves and pussywillow branches.

Colored pencil on white paper, 9 x 8½ in

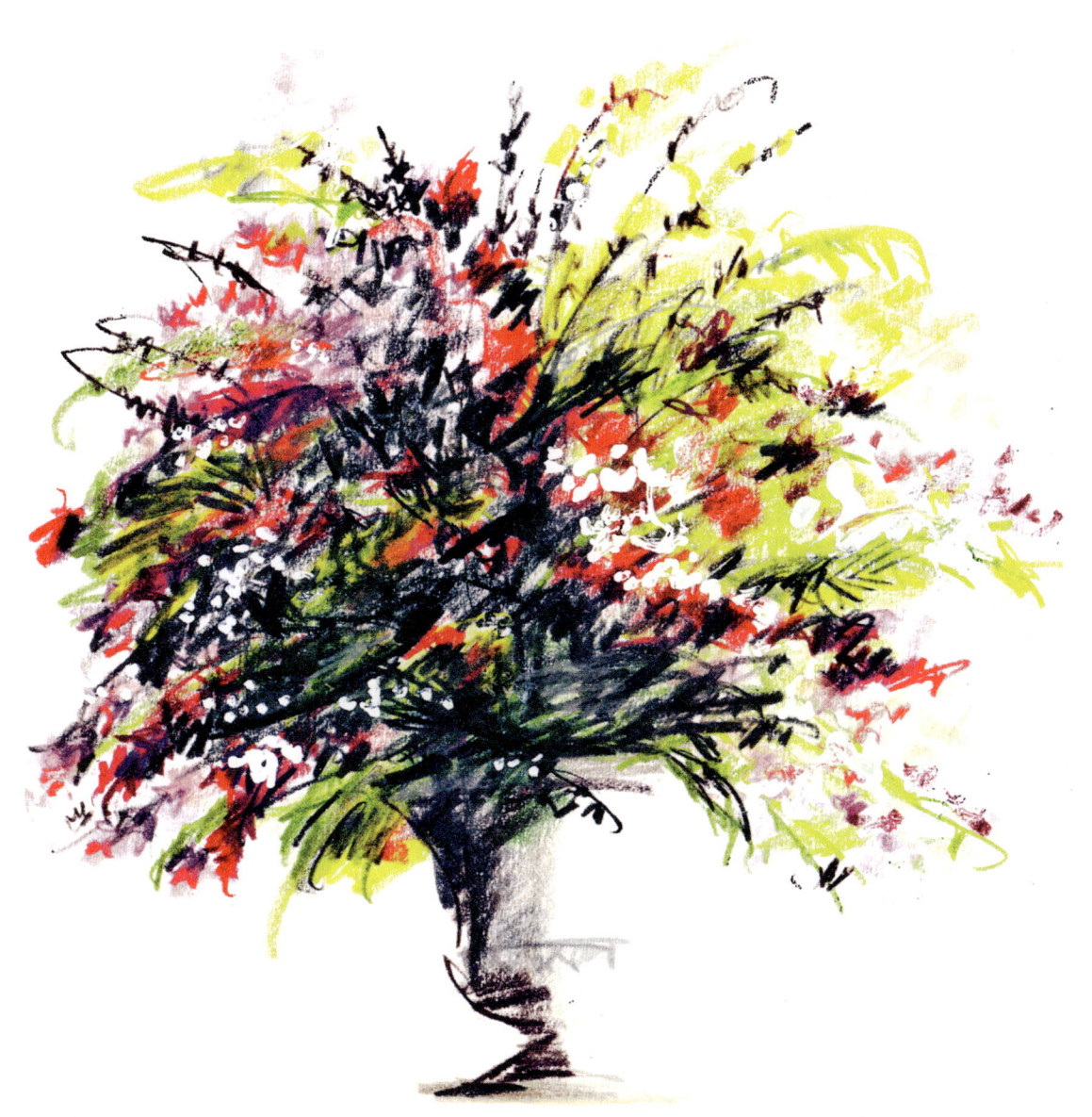

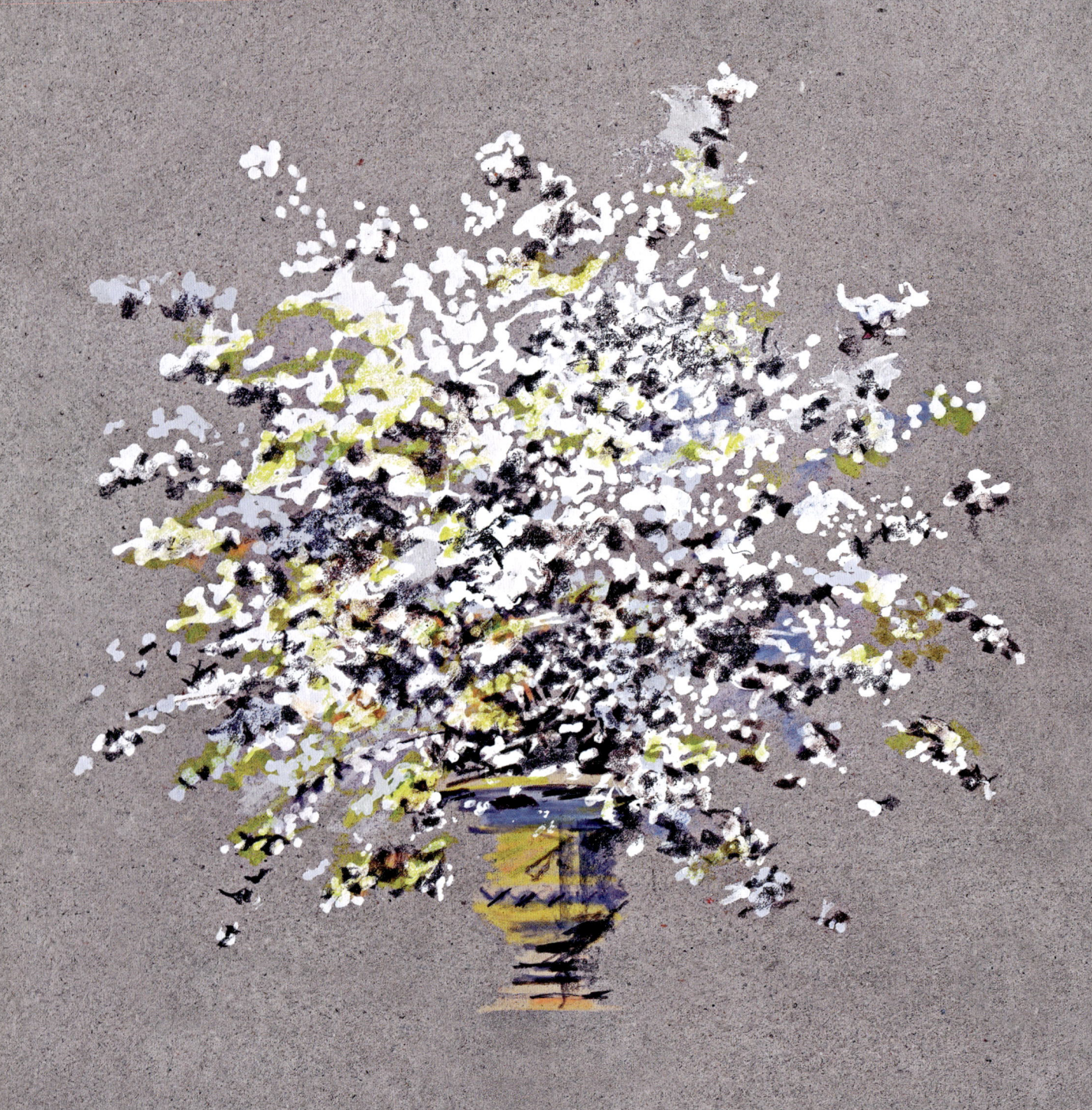

8 March:

Forced apple blossoms. Usually appears in early spring.

Lots of whiteout with colored pencil on cardboard, 8⅞ x 8¼ in

11 March:

Colored pencil on cardboard, 7 x 7 in

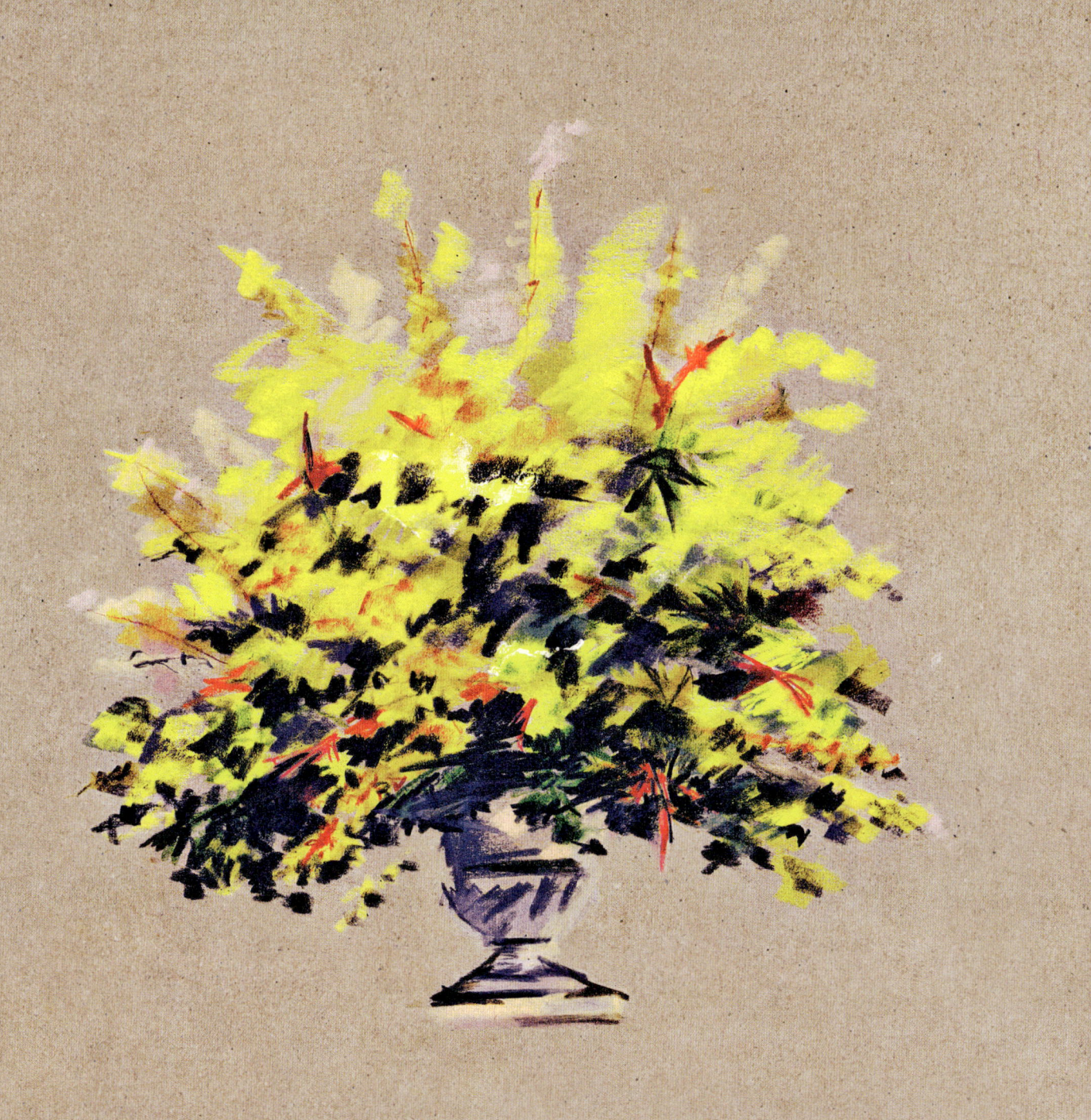

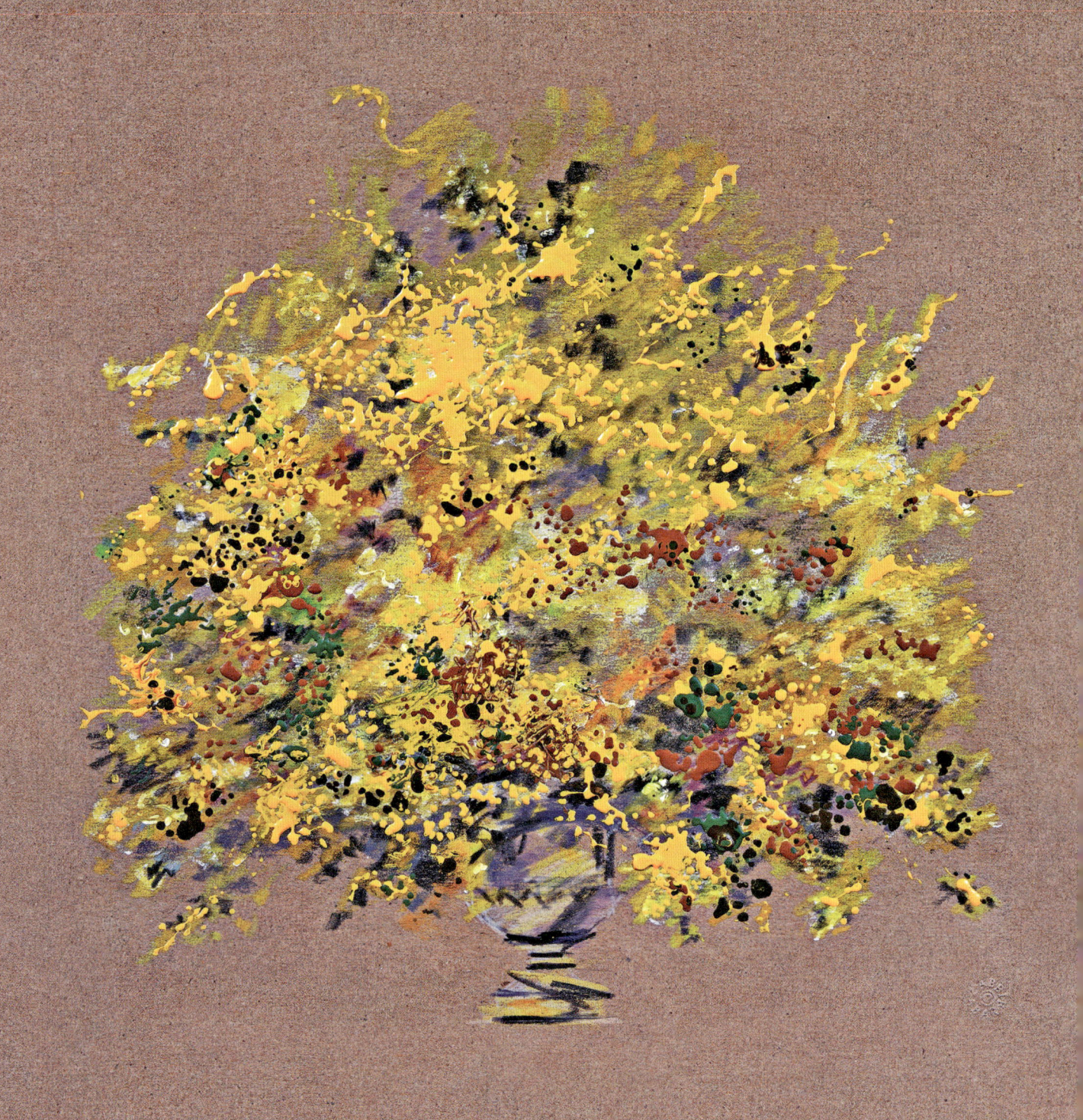

16 March:

Just forsythia branches. One of the most dramatic bouquets when all are blooming yellow, echoing the forsythia branches on the north side of the Met. Chris always said these were his favorite, so when I was asked by the Met to gift him one of my drawings, it was a no-brainer.

When approaching this morning, I could see the white tent that was being set up on the entry stairs ahead of tomorrow's opening-night gala for "Jacqueline Kennedy: The White House Years—Selections from the John F. Kennedy Library and Museum Costume Institute," which will run from 1 May to 29 July, 2001. It will be one of the Met's best-attended exhibits. I was thrilled when the guards suggested that I run upstairs before the doors open and catch the exhibit while the rooms were empty. I did.

Colored pencils on cardboard, 8⅞ x 9¼ in

29 March:

A haze of apple blossoms and cherry blossoms.

Colored pencil and whiteout on cardboard, 8½ x 7⅝ in

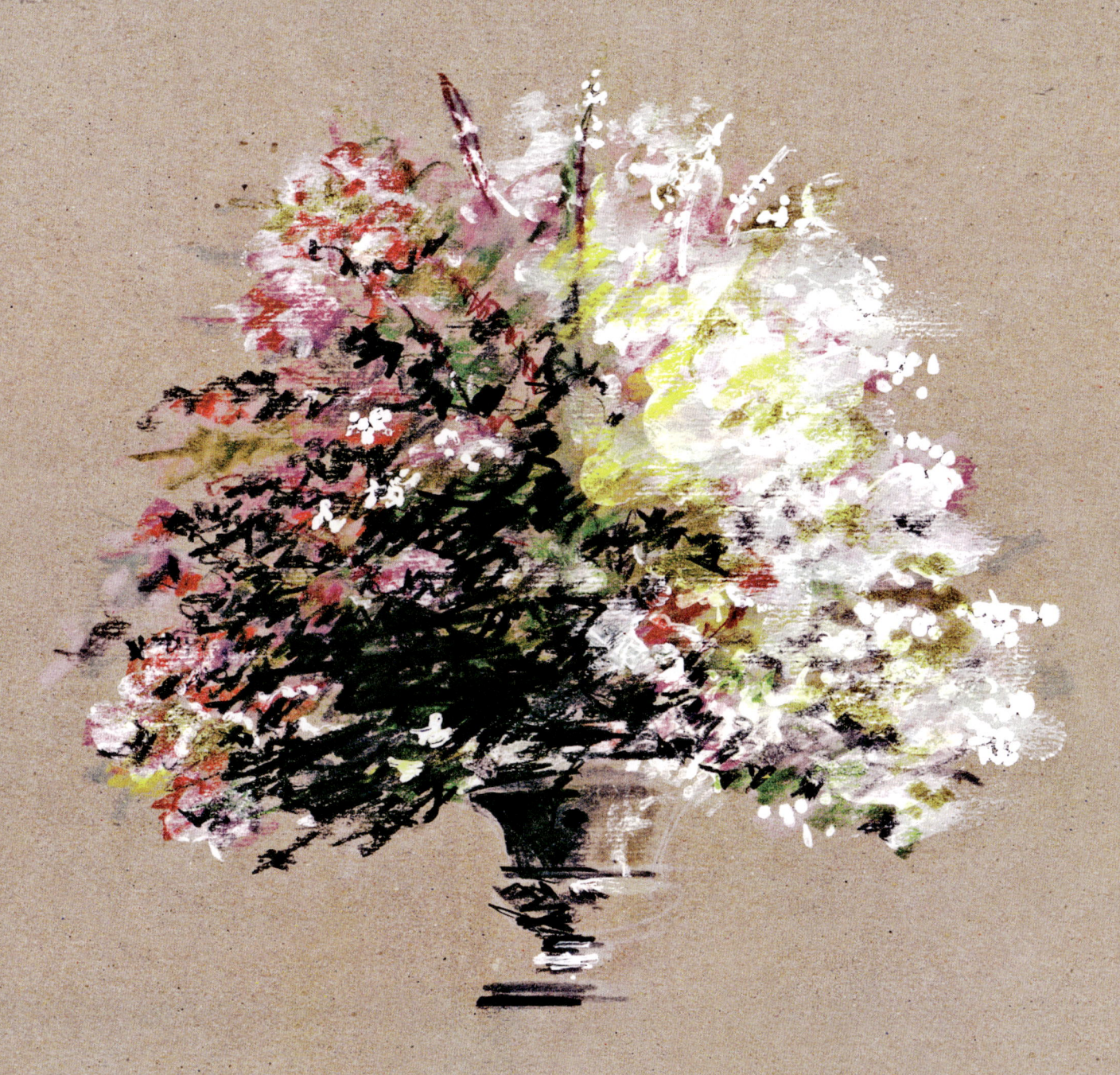

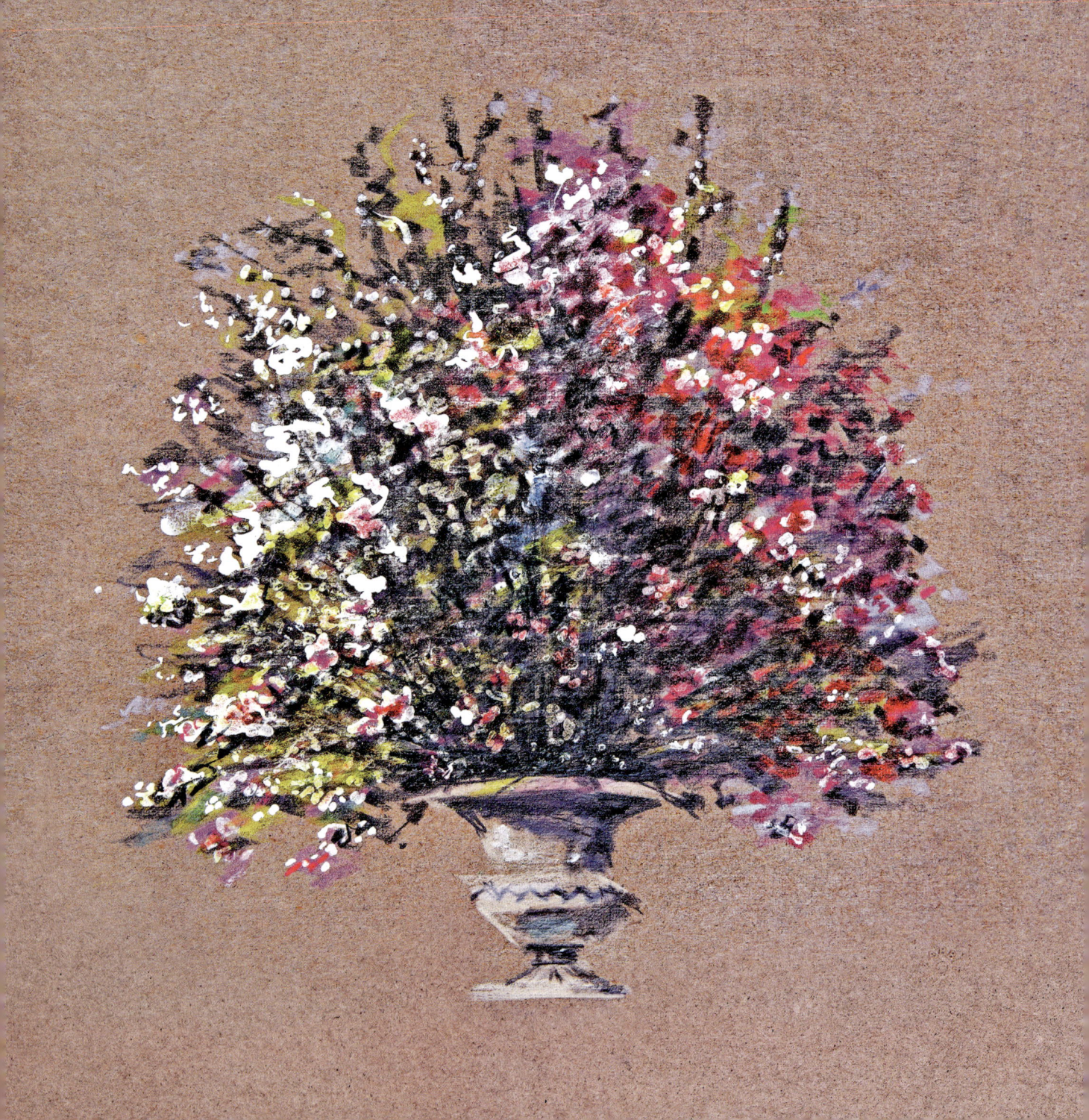

13–14 April:

Dogwood branches with pussywillow.

Colored pencil and whiteout on cardboard, 7⅞ x 8¼ in

14 April:

One of my favorite arrangements. Just dogwood branches. What else do you need? This was sold to someone I knew and when he died, I bought it back from his estate before it went up for auction. Does every artist have the need to collect back their favorites?

Mostly whiteout with some colored pencil on cardboard, 8¾ x 9¾ in

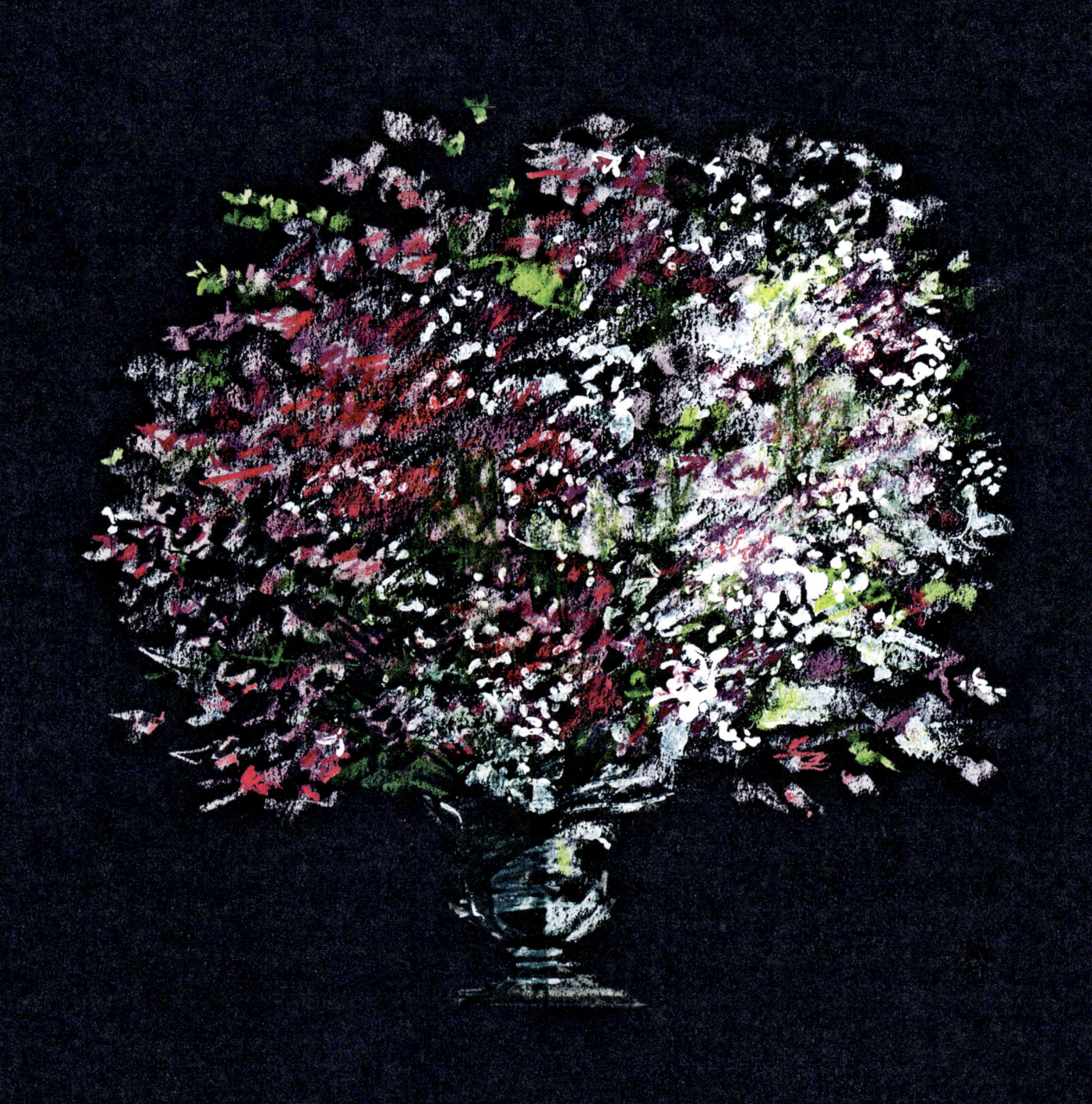

19 April:

Still intrigued by drawing bouquets on a black background.

Colored pencil and whiteout on black paper, 8⅝ x 7½ in

4 May:

Very showy. Birds of paradise, palm fronds, and banana leaves.

Colored pencil on cardboard, 7 x 7 in

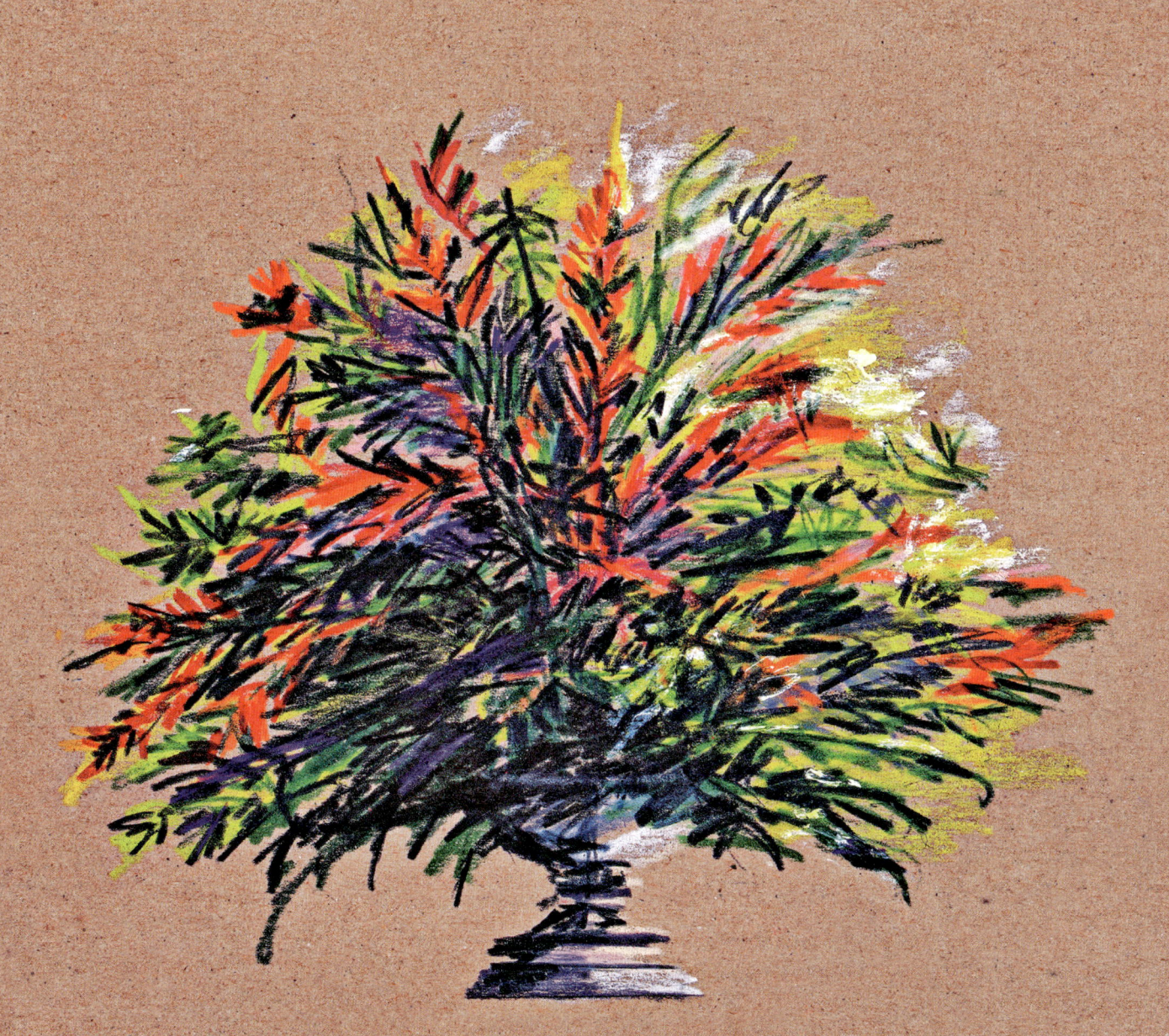

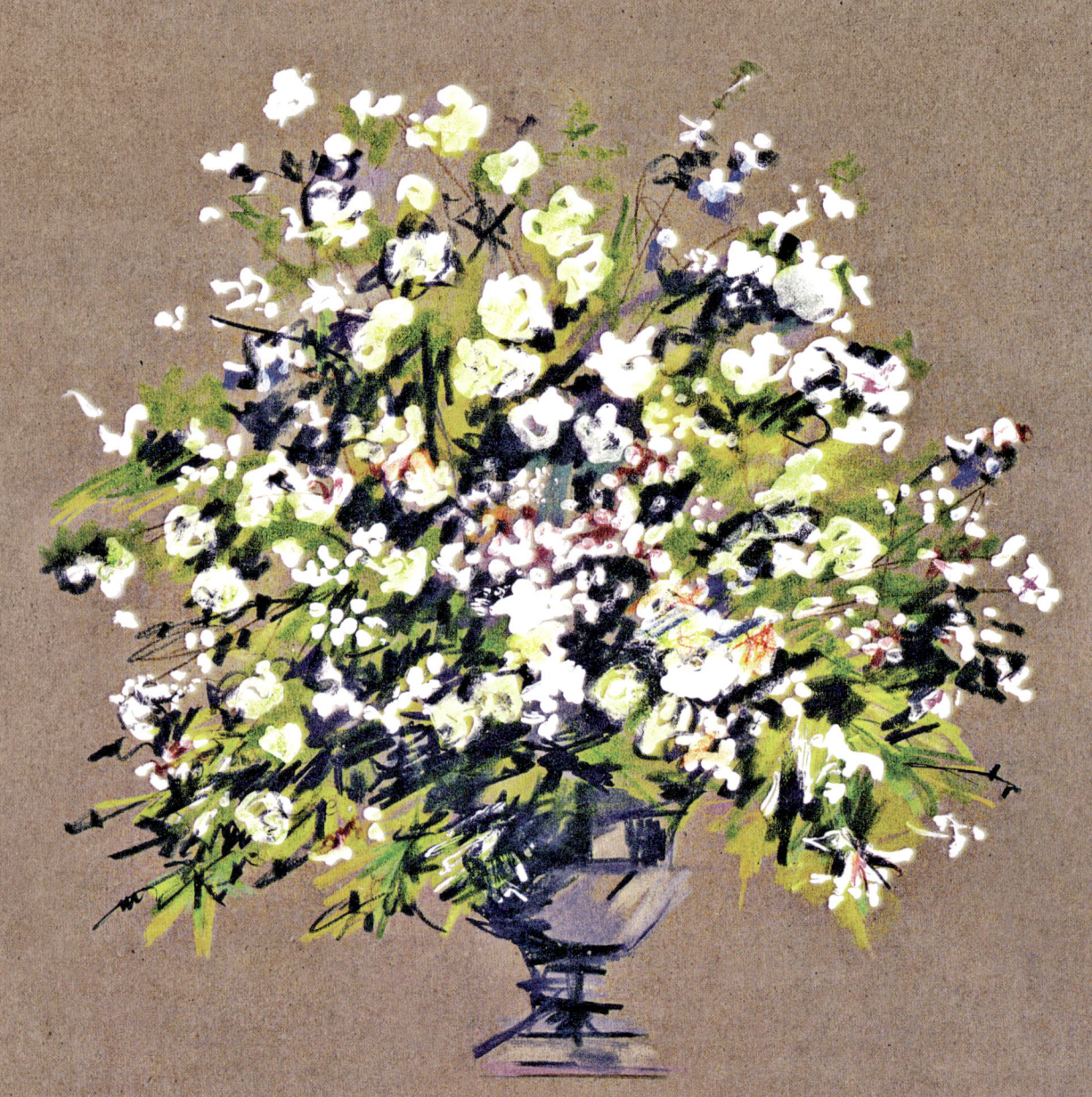

14 May:

Small puff balls of hydrangeas.

Colored pencil and whiteout on cardboard, 7 x 7¾ in

18 May:

It's 8:30 a.m.—a very late start for me—and the Great Hall is noisy. The arrangement is tight and formal, with hydrangeas and some azaleas, but I like the chiaroscuro challenge it presents. A big crowd is huddled, waiting to get in the entry doors to keep dry. It's been pouring for a week. The Head of Operations tells coat check guards, "Lots of snakes, again." I learn that this is guard-speak for how to arrange the crowd control stanchions when it's raining cats and dogs. I make sure this drawing on paper is well-wrapped before I leave.

Colored pencil on white rag paper, 9⅝ x 9 in

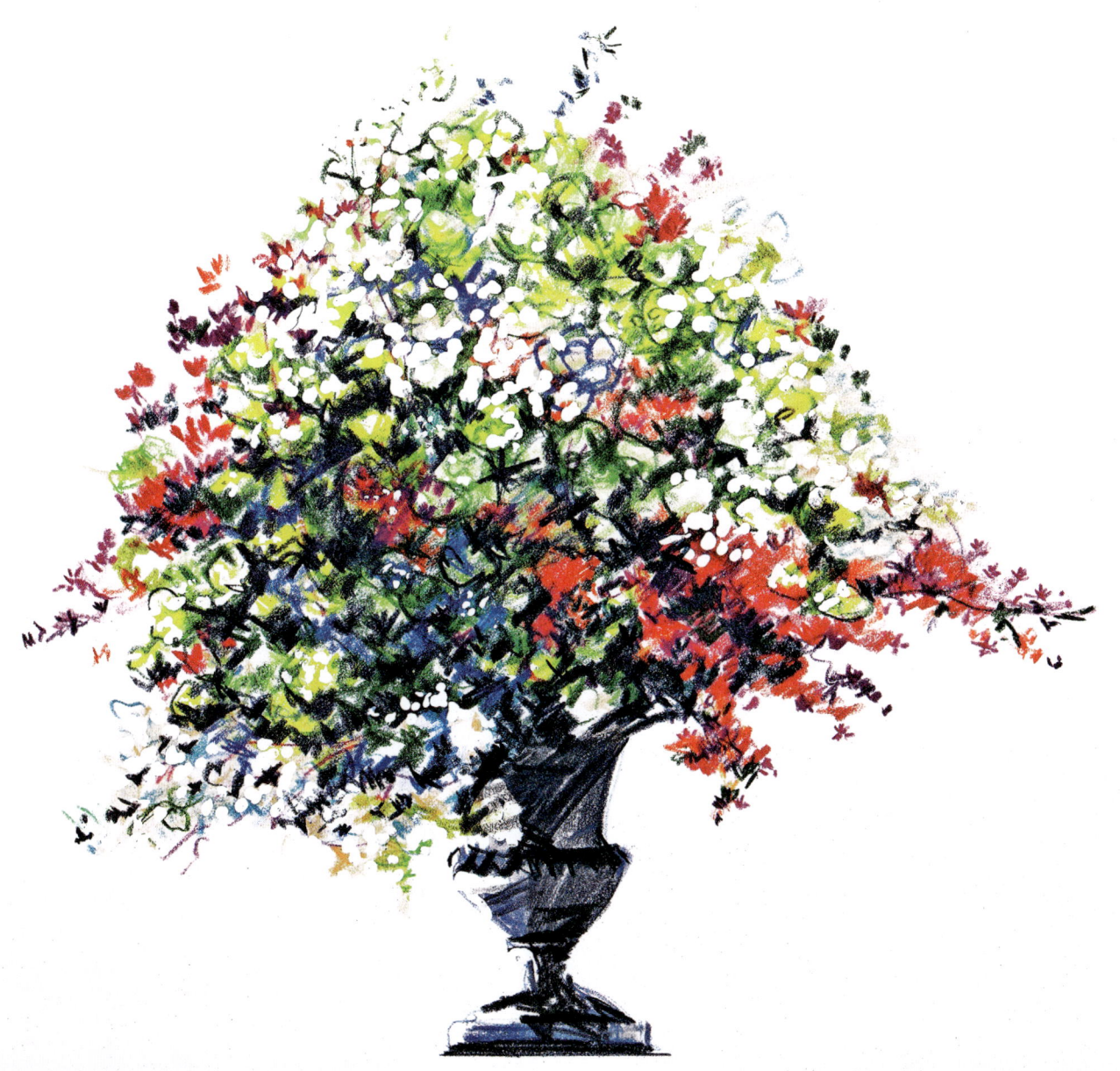

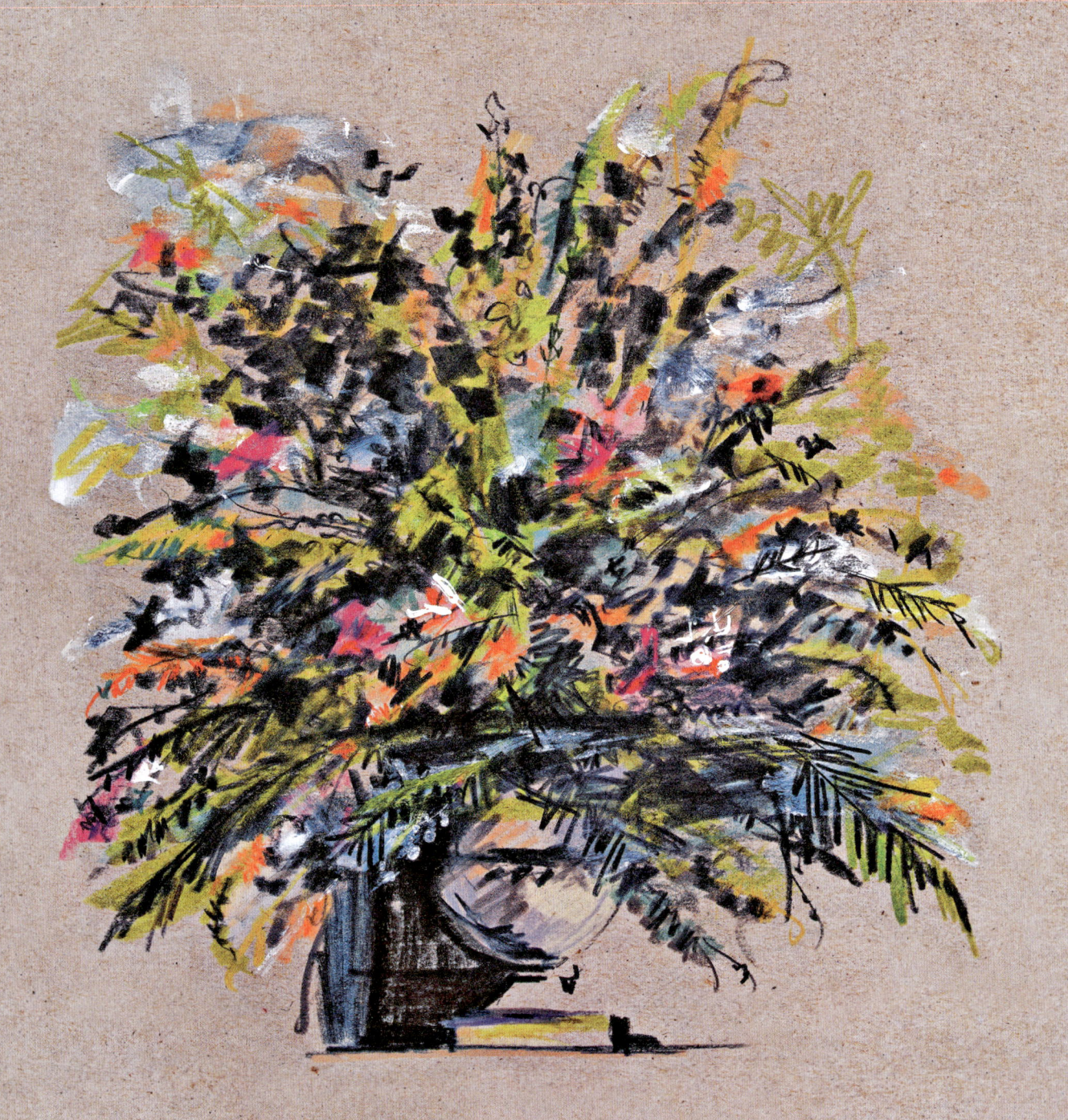

28 May:

Apricot-colored *Agastache*, with wide low-hanging palm fronds and big white *Allium* heads. I was in the mood to highlight the urn by adding a black shadow behind it for once.

Colored pencil and whiteout on cardboard, 7⅝ x 8½ in

Summer

Of course, Summer bouquets, not relying on any filler, could be the most floral. In the mind's eye, high-summer bouquets summoned up familiar fields of sunflowers, and *Helichrysum* (also in the sunflower family). There were huge purple chive blossoms, most likely much bigger than anything you could grow in your own garden. Mixed in with the ongoing profusion of lilies, there were the unfamiliar tropical blooms such as the bird-of-paradise flowers in the *Strelitzia* genus.

8 June:

Yellow and white lilies, palm fronds, those stately *Eremurus* (much taller than anything in your own garden), *Dracaena* leaves, small hydrangea puff balls.

Colored pencil with lots of whiteout on cardboard, 8 in (almost square)

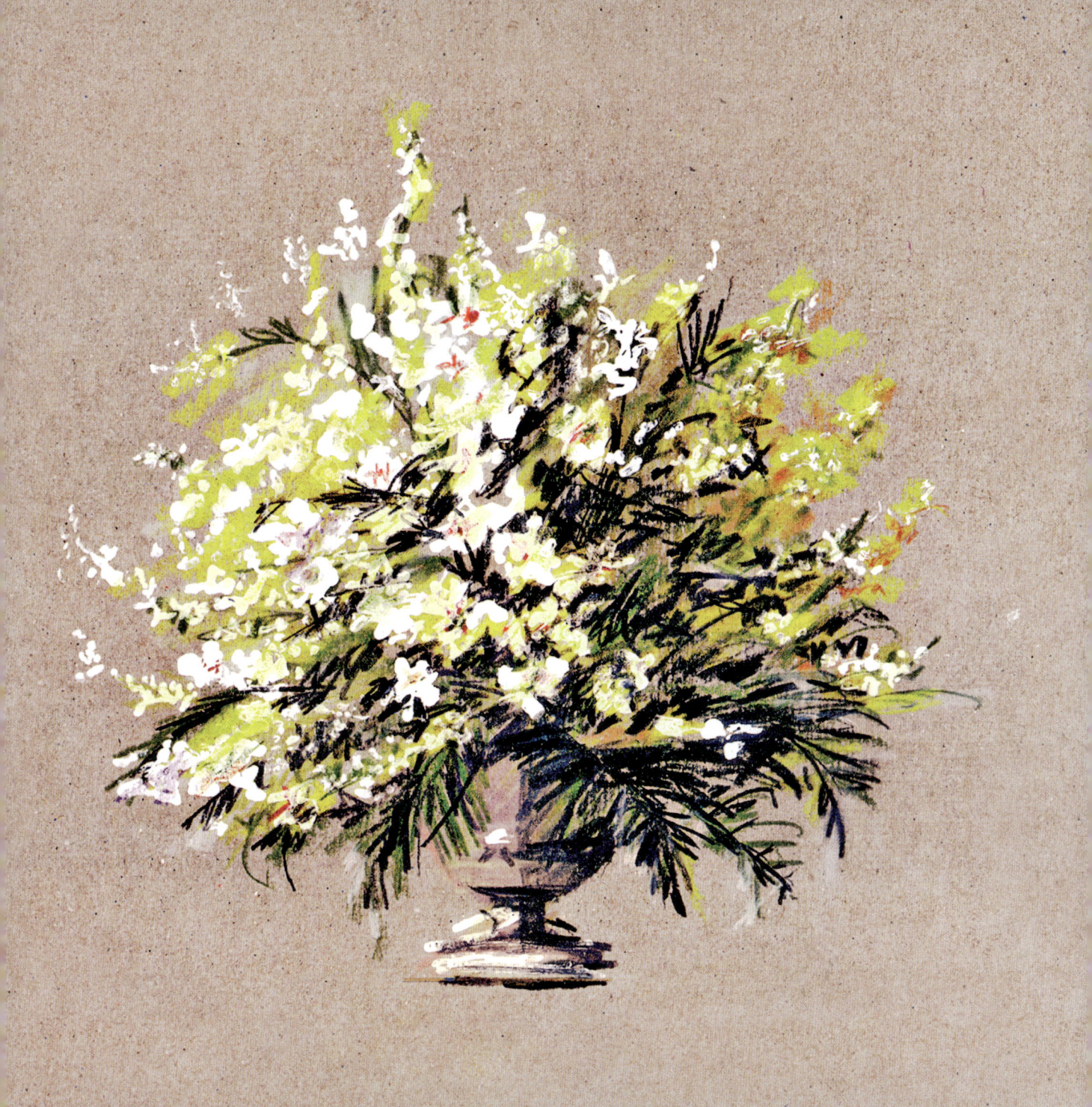

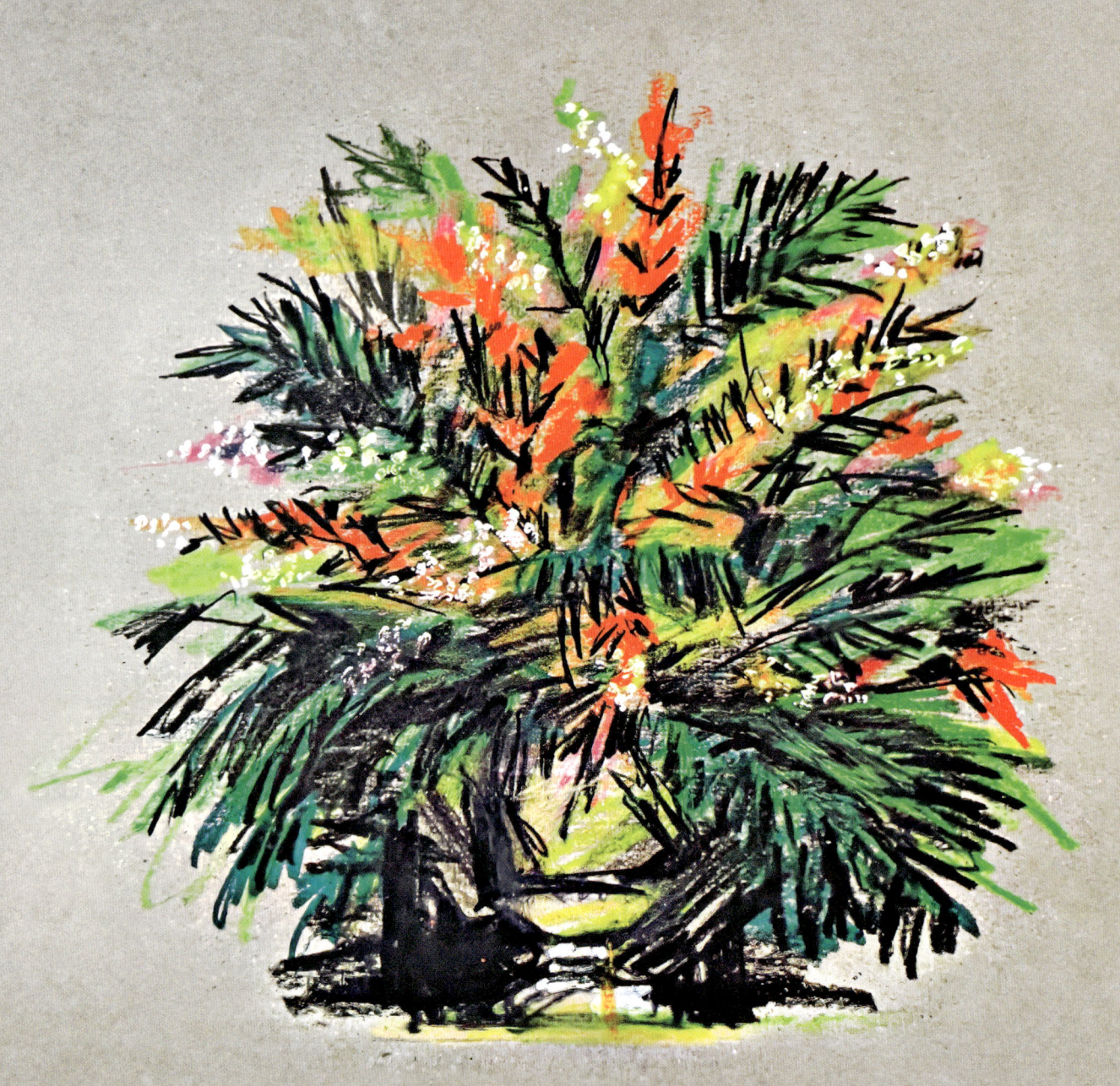

23 June:

Big palms and other startling, oversized leaves.

Colored pencil on cardboard, 7¾ x 8½ in

24 June:

A very full bouquet; the essence of summer in bloom, including squiggly shoots of yellow and apricot *Eremurus*, white lilies (with orange stamens not yet removed, adding good color for me but staining for them) and small sunflowers that never opened. There are branches of privet with white flowers, reminiscent of the flowering privet hedges in the Hamptons at this time of year. There are flowering thistles with mauve heads, plus deep-maroon smoke puffs, woodland ferns, meadow rue, clematis, *Crocosmia*, *Agastache*, red-hot pokers, fountain grass, *Monarda*, poppies, and of course lilies.

Colored pencil on white paper, 7¼ x 9⅛ in

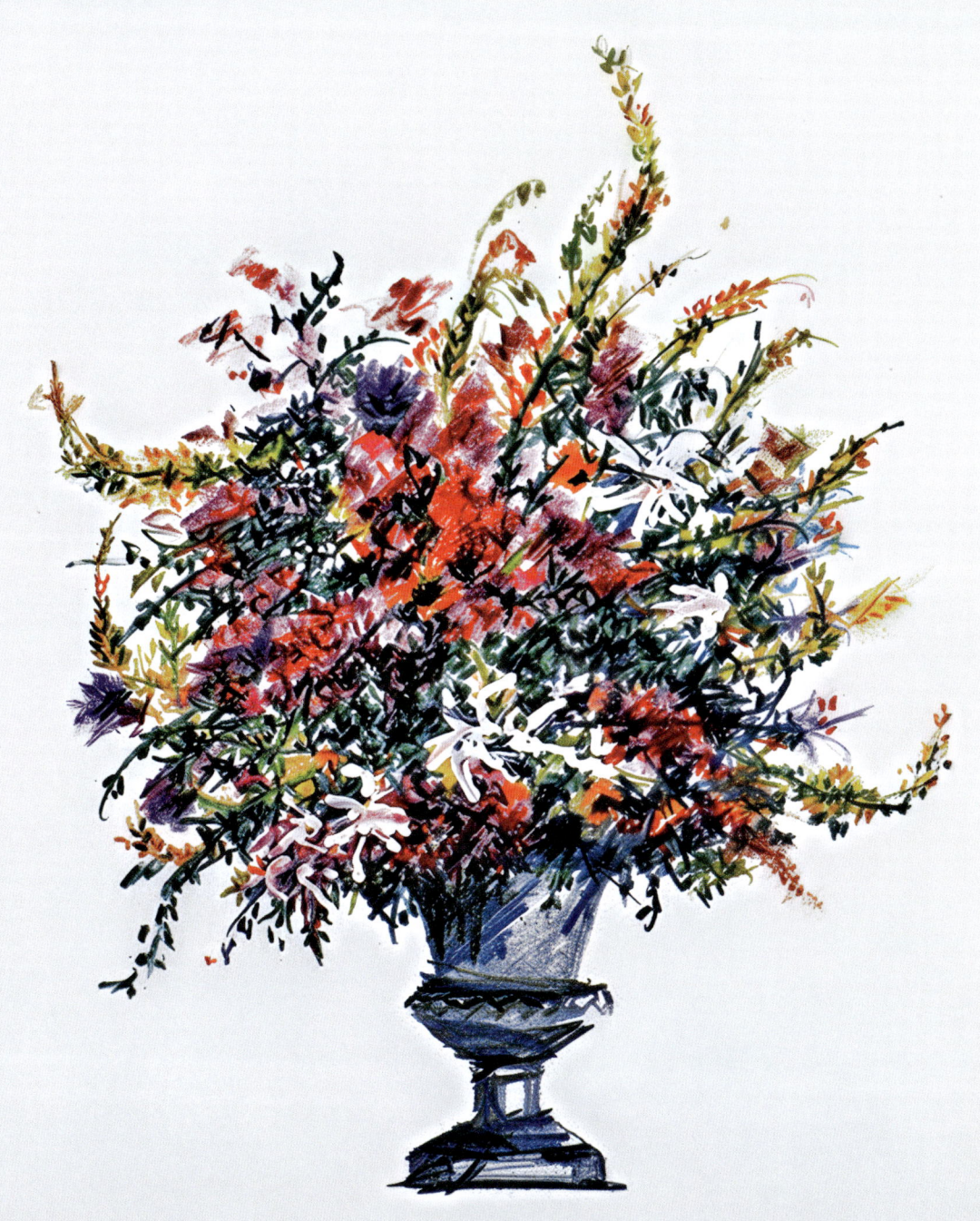

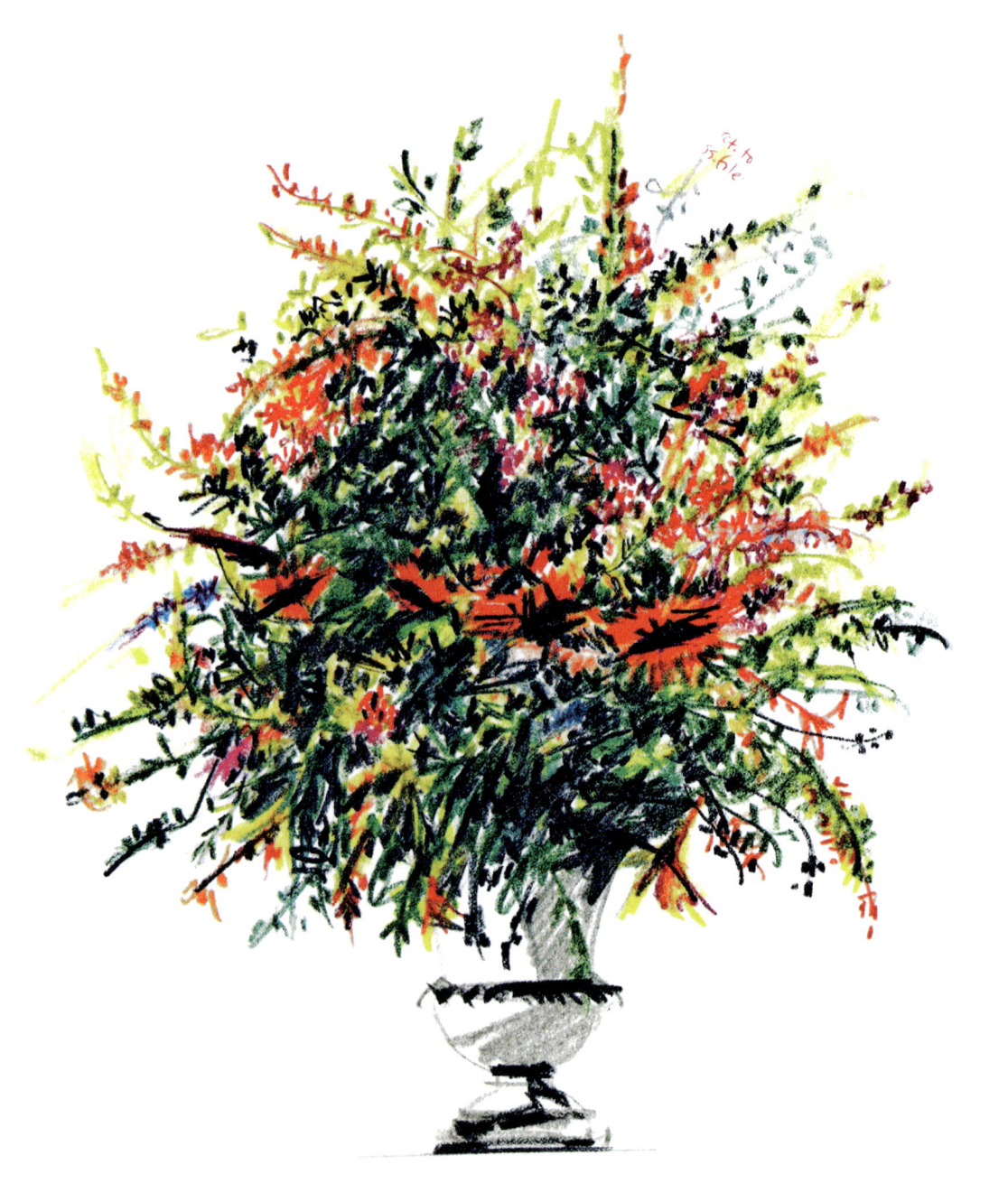

28 June:

Cattails, aromatic lilies, grape leaves, oak leaves, *Rhododendron* leaves, tuberoses, *Viburnum* berries but predominantly huge happy sunflowers.

Colored pencil on paper, 8 x 8¾ in

11 July:

For the first time, I'm noticing that *Eremurus* open from the bottom upwards, and that's a good thing because they will not block the bold, purple chive blossoms. Lots of branches with brilliant yellow-green leaves at the top of the arrangement.

Colored pencil on cardboard, 7⅛ x 7½ in (re-cut to square it off)

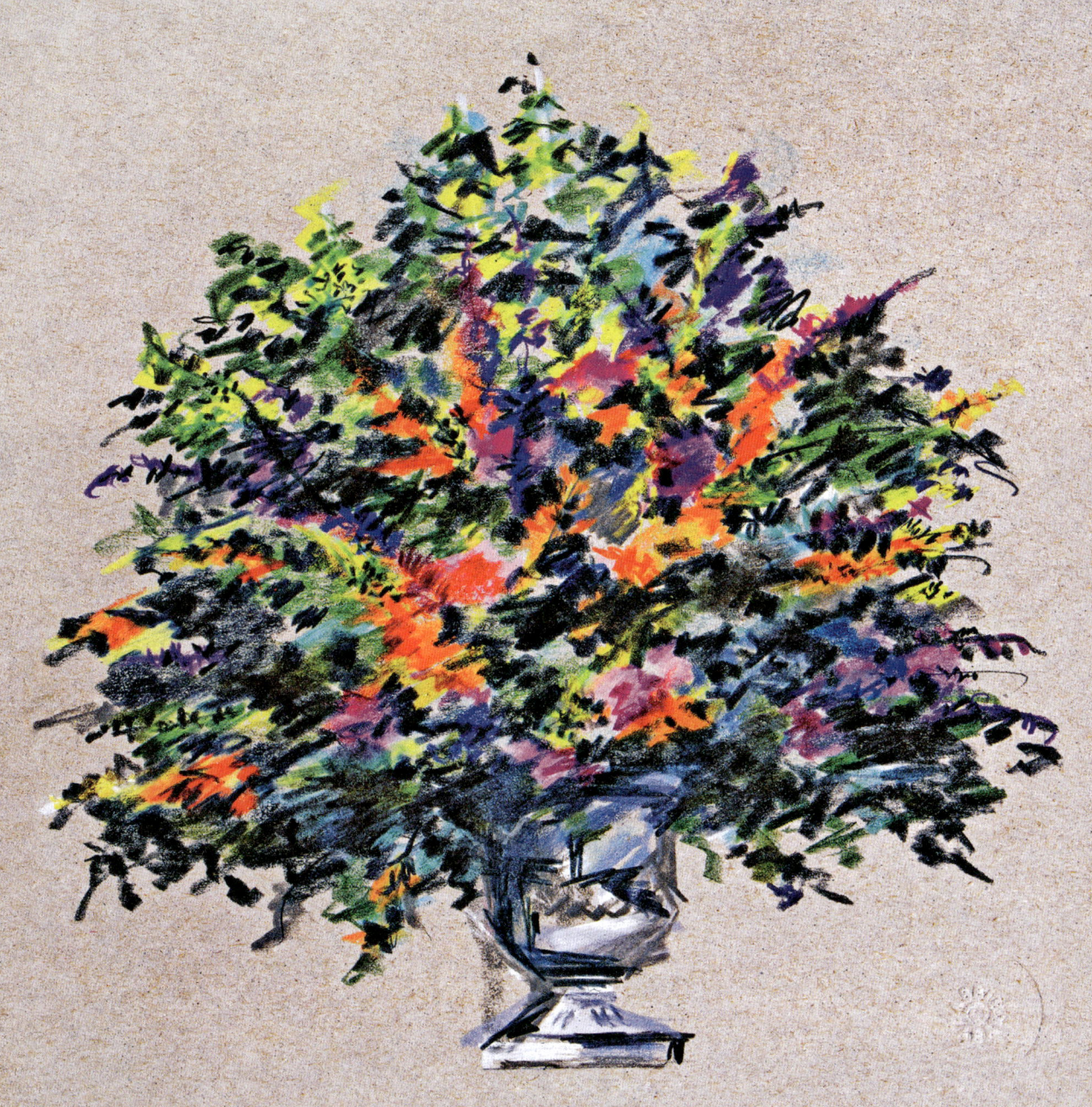

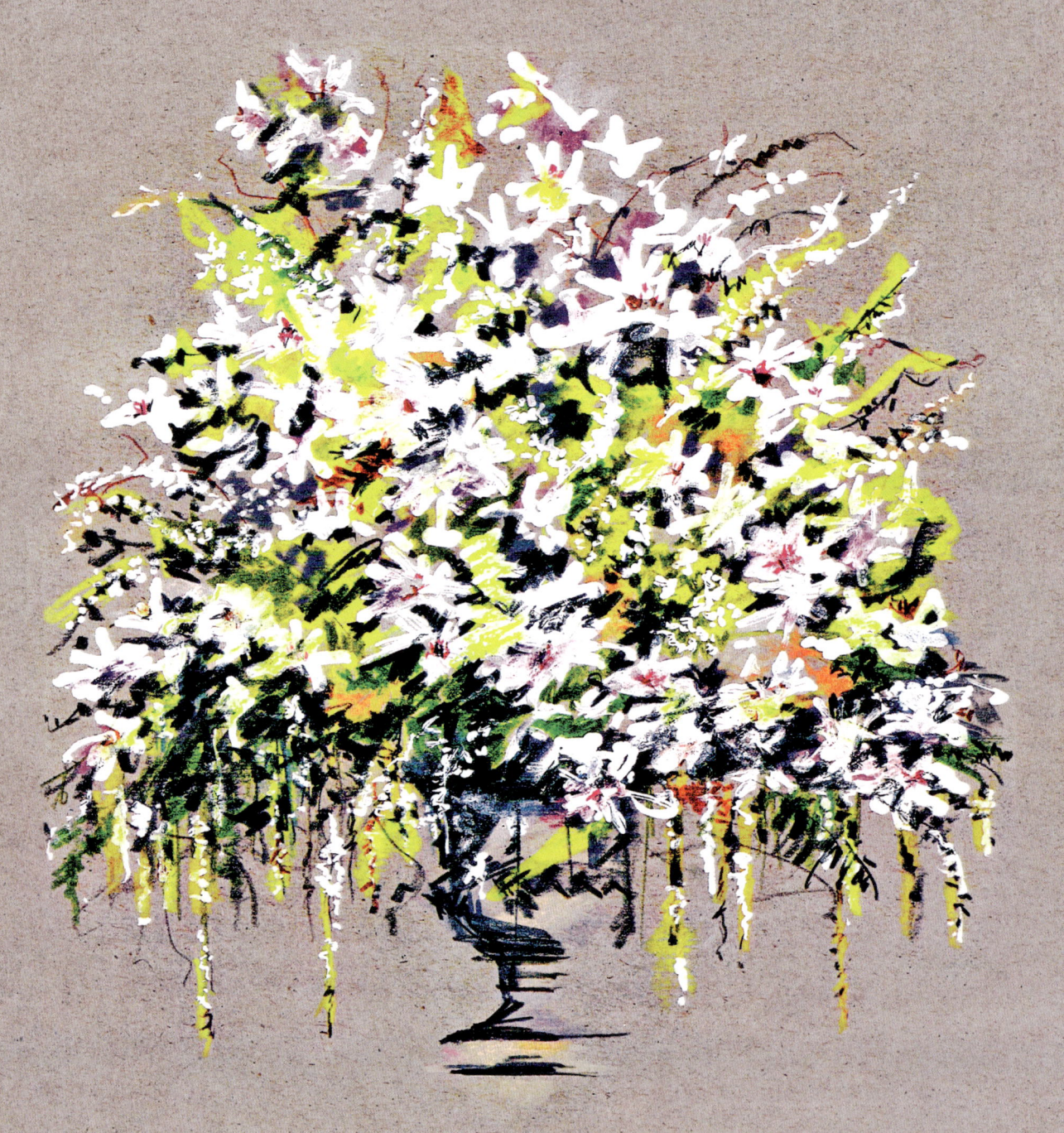

17–18 July:

Almost all lilies (with pink stamens that haven't been removed), but there's a base of palm leaves and an understory of dripping white panicles of *Wisteria*, slowly fading to pink and green—my favorite dripping bouquet.

Colored pencil and whiteout on cardboard, 9 x 8 in

21 July:

Trying colored pencil and whiteout on three-ply black board, 7¼ x 6¾ in

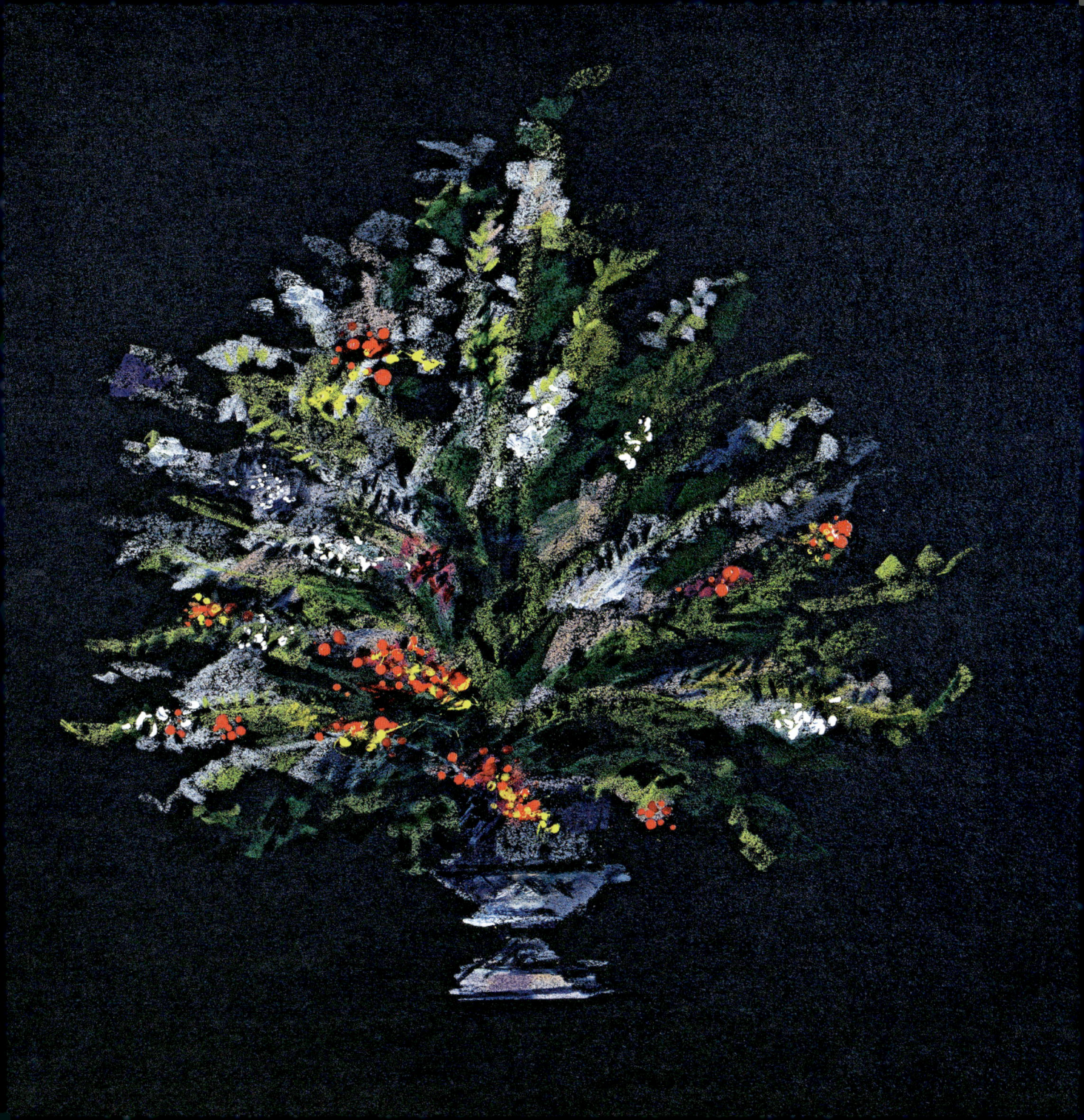

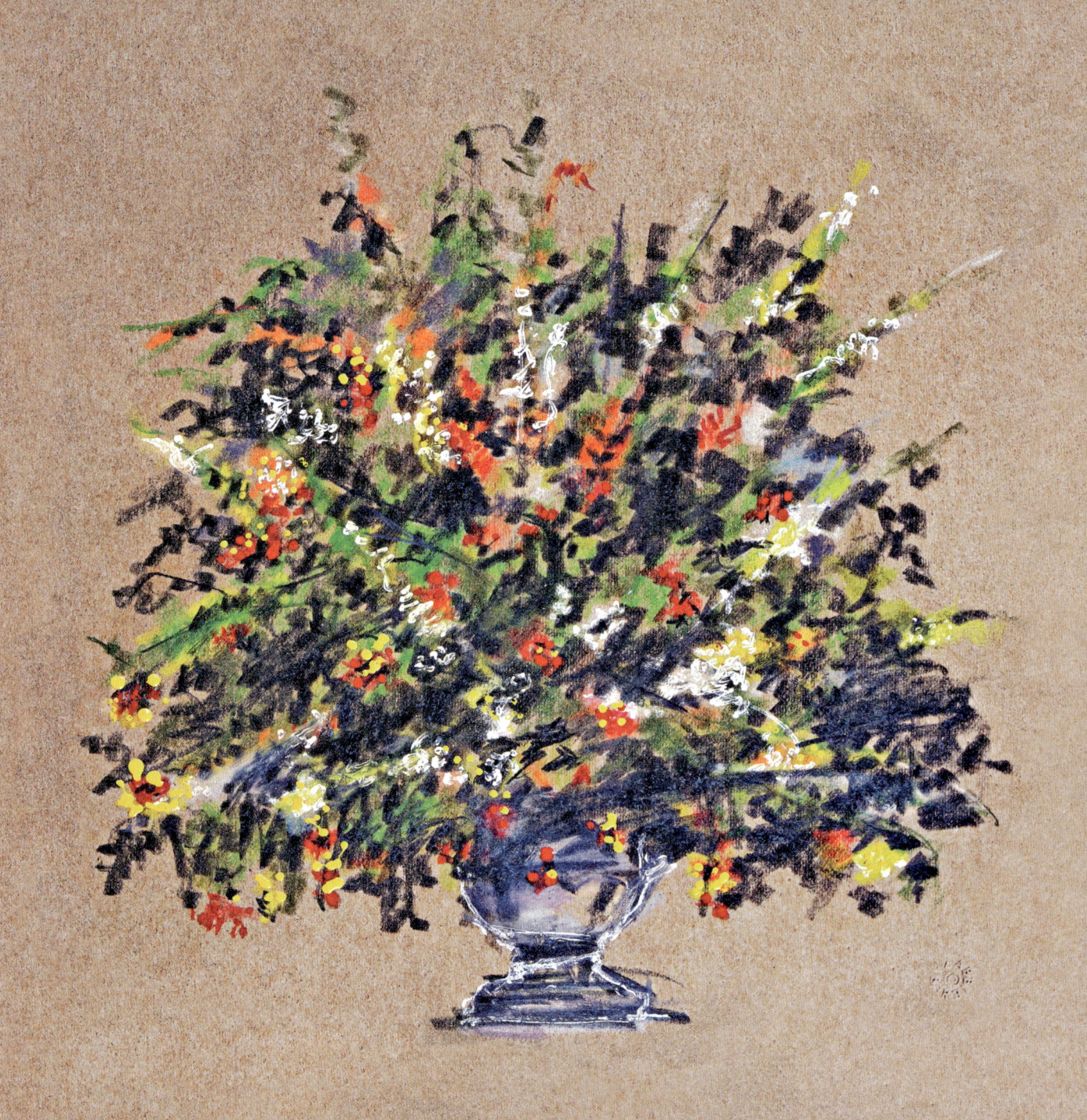

29 July:

Eremurus grape leaves; yellow, red, and orange berries. I outlined the urn with whiteout.

Colored pencil and whiteout on cardboard, 7¾ x 8⅜ in

12 August:

Tall, dramatic sprays of *Gladiolus*, grasses and *Eucalyptus*, with some branches of boxwood at the base.

Colored pencil on darker cardboard with whiteout, 8⅜ x 8½ in

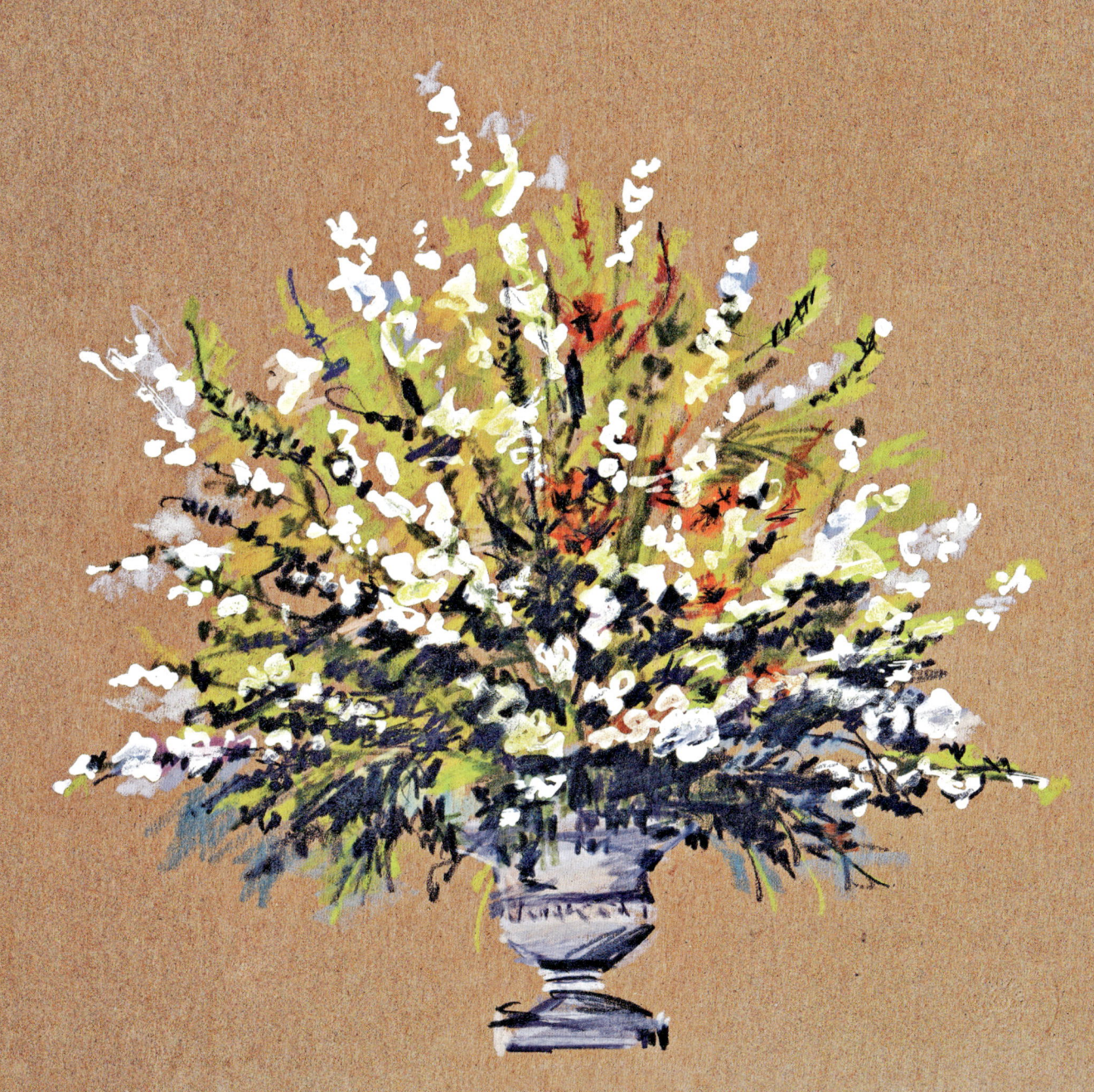

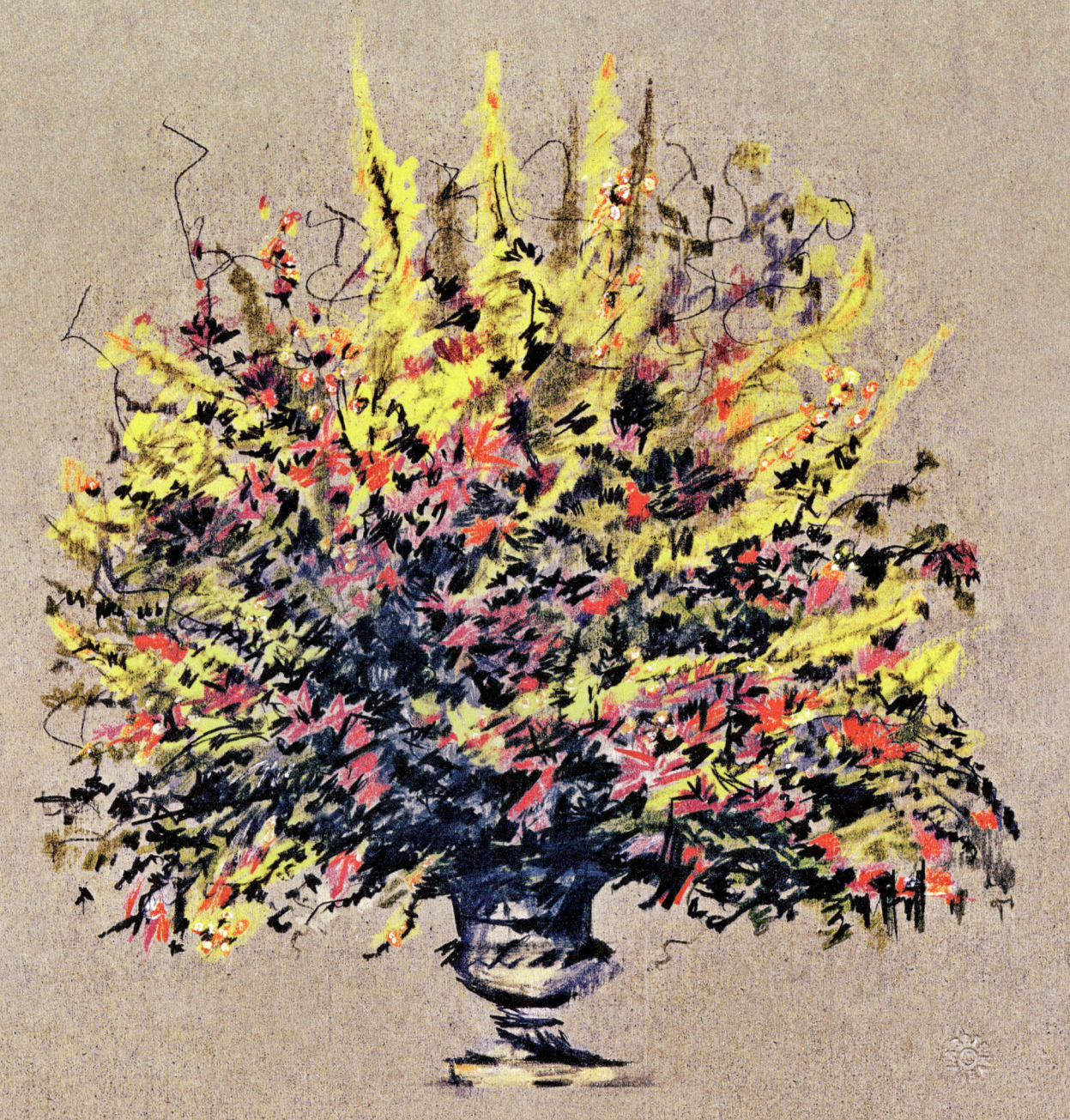

20 August:

Lilies, green leaves, *Eucalyptus*, *Eremurus*.

Colored pencil on cardboard, 8⅜ x 9½ in

22 August:

Mostly orange daylilies. Chartreuse pom poms; fading orange *Gladiolus*; branches of berries and curly willow; white scented lilies; *Euonymus* leaves. And lots of flyaway branches.

Colored pencil on white paper, 5⅞ x 5⅞ in

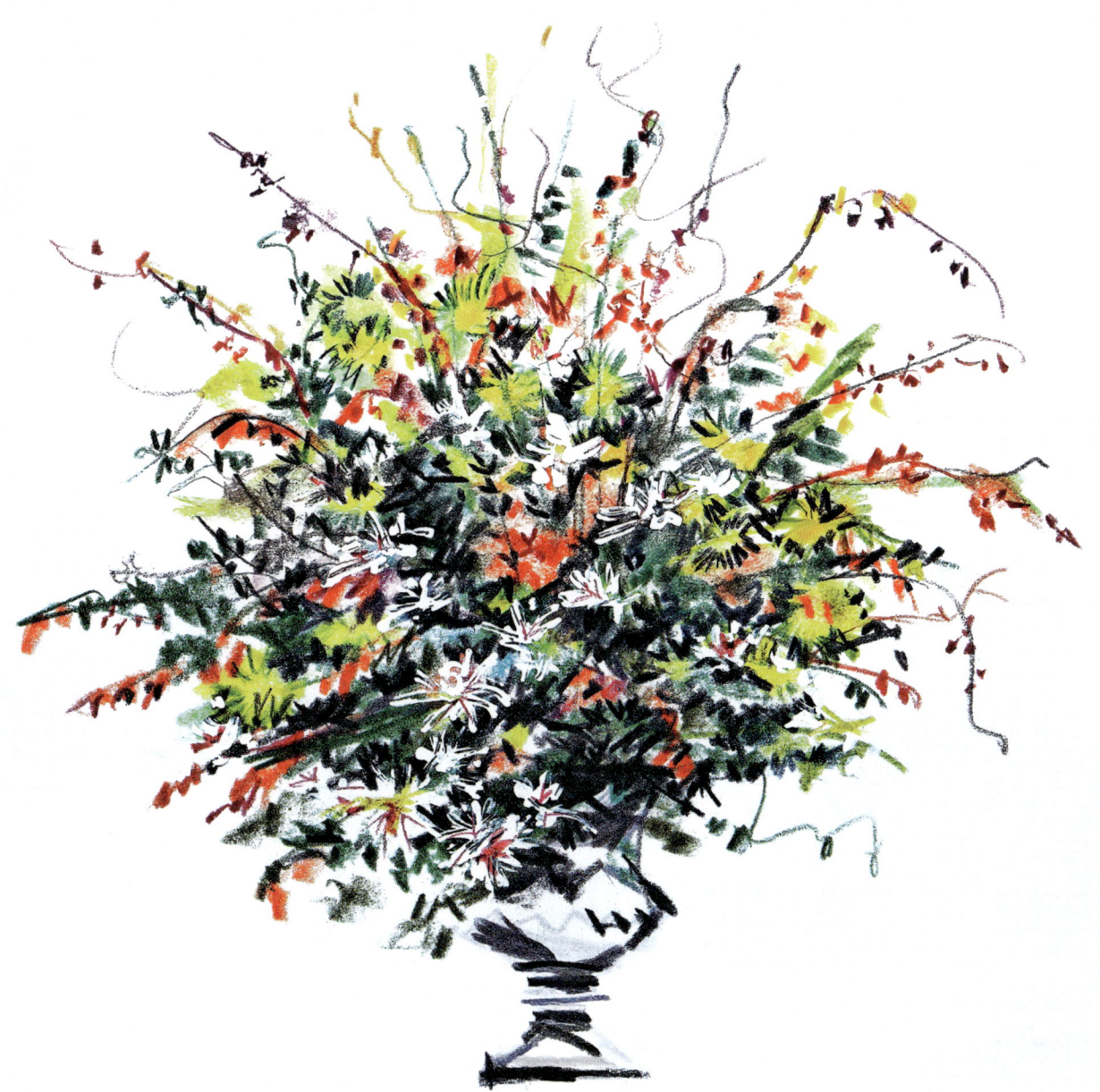

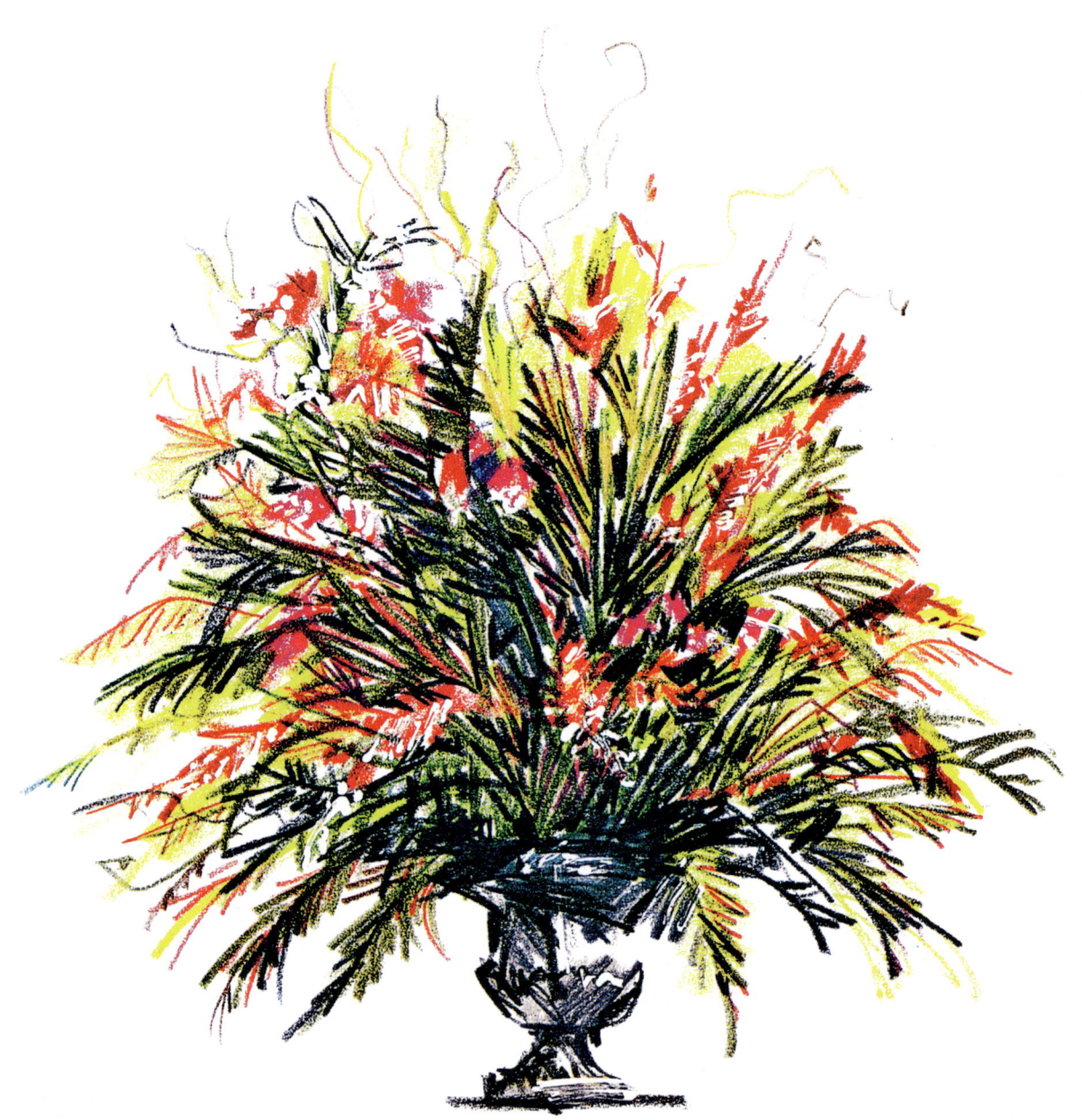

28 August:

Bird-of-paradise flowers; palm leaves; thin, green willow branches, exotic red flowers, similar to lupines, turning to puffy pink flowers when they opened.

Colored pencil on white paper, 6 x 6 in

Fall

Fall bouquets had autumn foliage with earthy colors and all the berries that the birds had missed. Branches of evergreens, such as *Rhododendra*, were introduced, and there were lilies almost any time of year. Closer to the holidays, shiny dark-green leaves of *Magnolia grandiflora* with furry brown felted undersides joined winterberry holly stems in hinting at the festivities without the need for a tree in the Great Hall. No reason to compete with the museum's traditional 20-ft blue spruce located in the Medieval Sculpture Hall, where it is surrounded by an 18th-century Neapolitan nativity scene with lifelike figures, silk-robed angels and Christmas music.

10 September:

I was there too early; not enough light. Then one of the guards put the spotlight on a bouquet that I was drawing. *Thank him,* I thought, *but remember you do not have to draw it as you see it.* Huge puffs of hydrangeas, magnolia leaves, and pink lilies. I eliminated all but the hydrangeas from my drawing.

Colored pencil and lots of whiteout on cardboard, 8½ x 8⅝ in

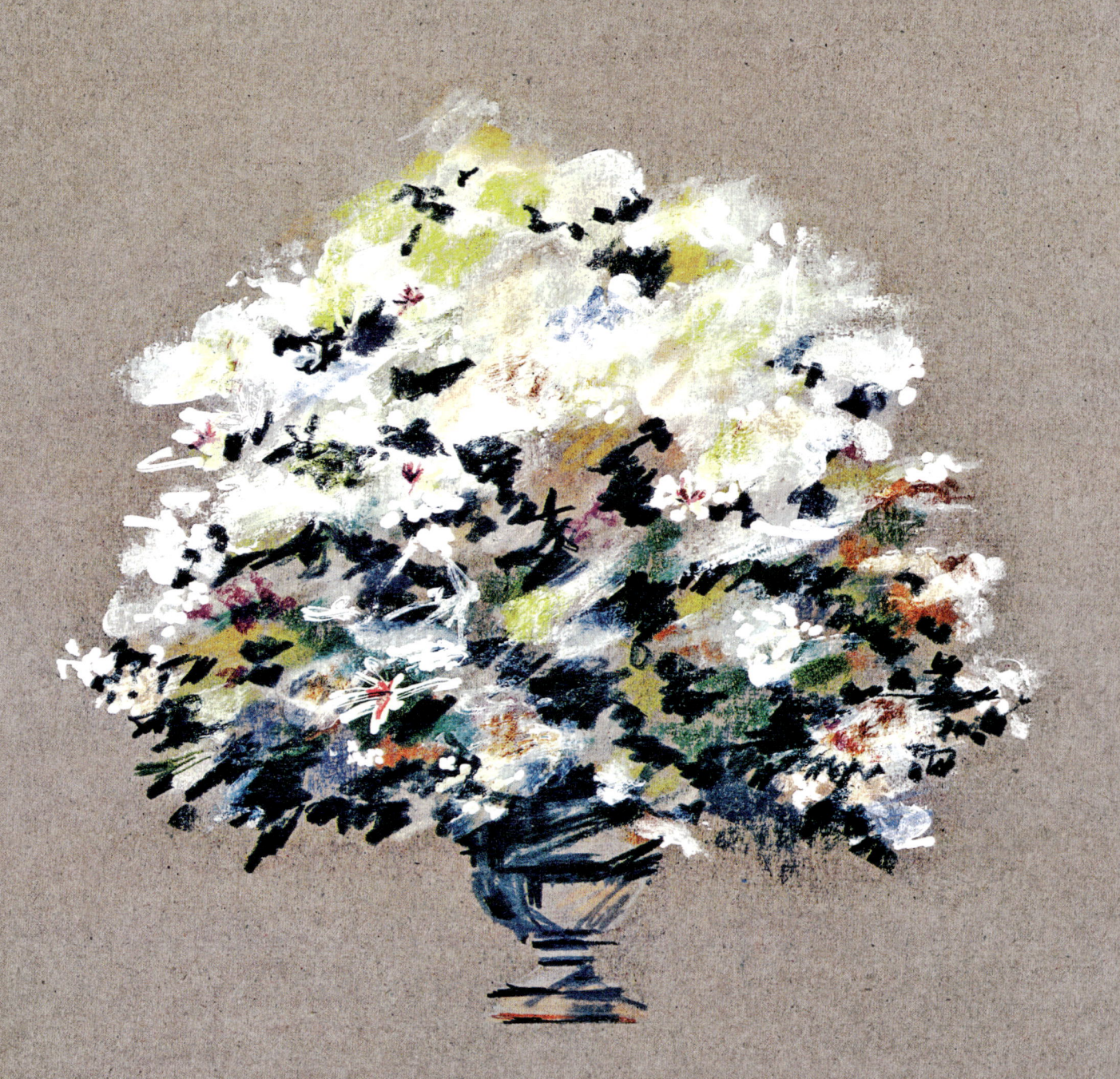

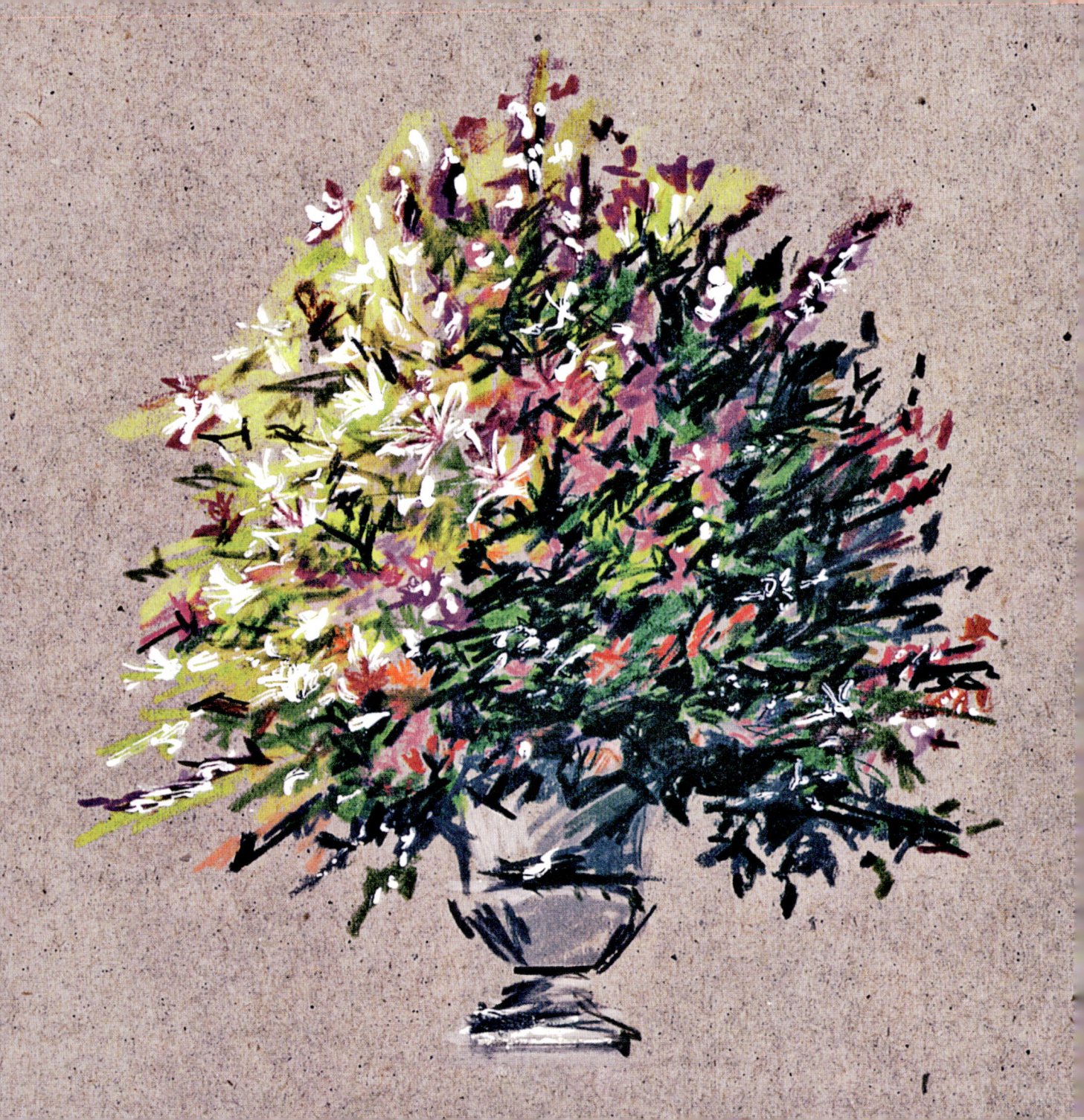

11 September:

Lots of lilies. My first donated, framed drawing.
It was auctioned at the Wave Hill public garden in the Bronx.

Colored pencil on cardboard, 6⅝ x 7⅝ in

12 September:

An overwhelming amount of palm fronds with hydrangeas, lilies, drippy pink-red furry things, white *Alliums* and red bromeliad flowers.

Colored pencil on white paper, 5⁵⁄₁₆ x 5⅜ in

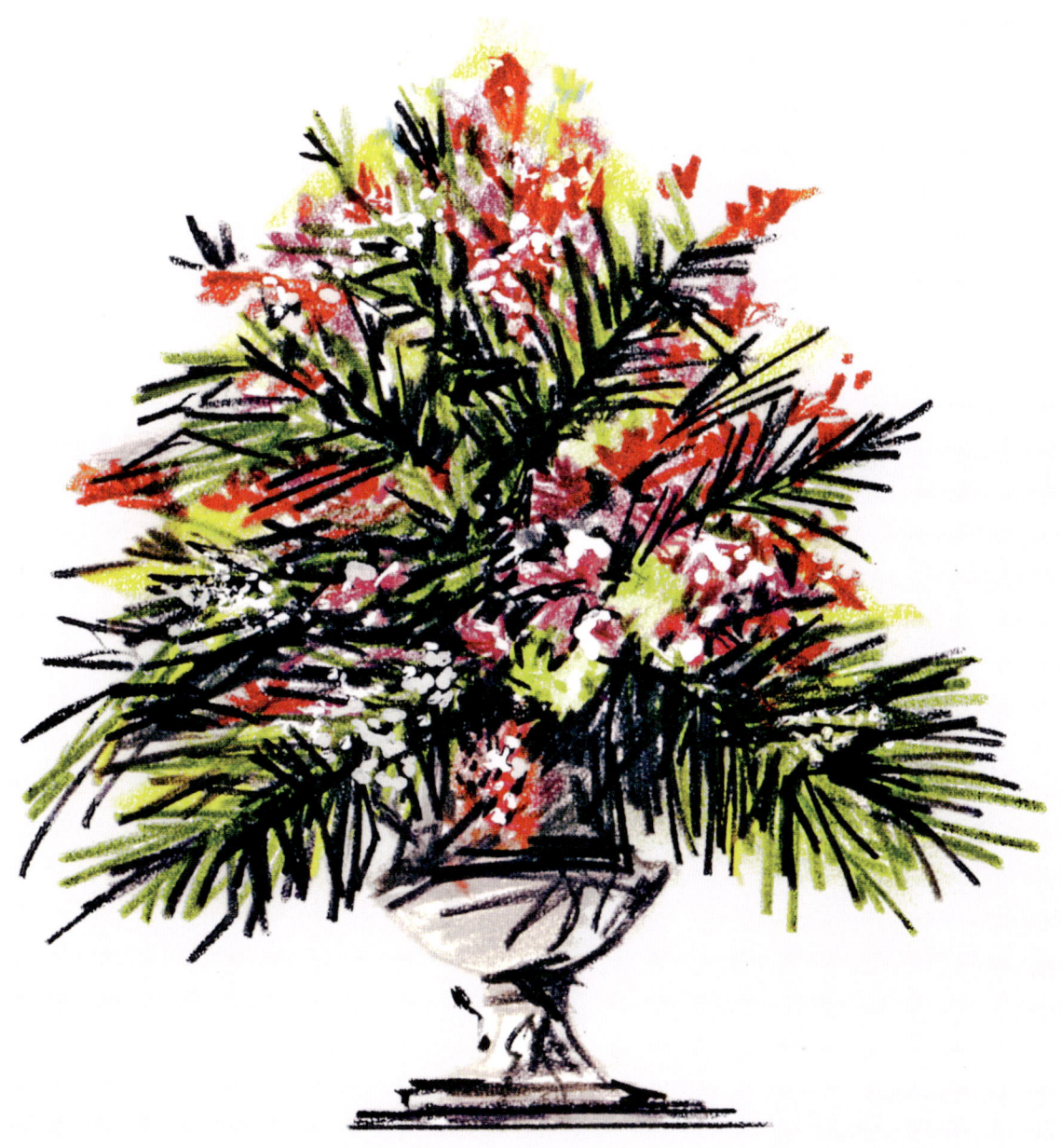

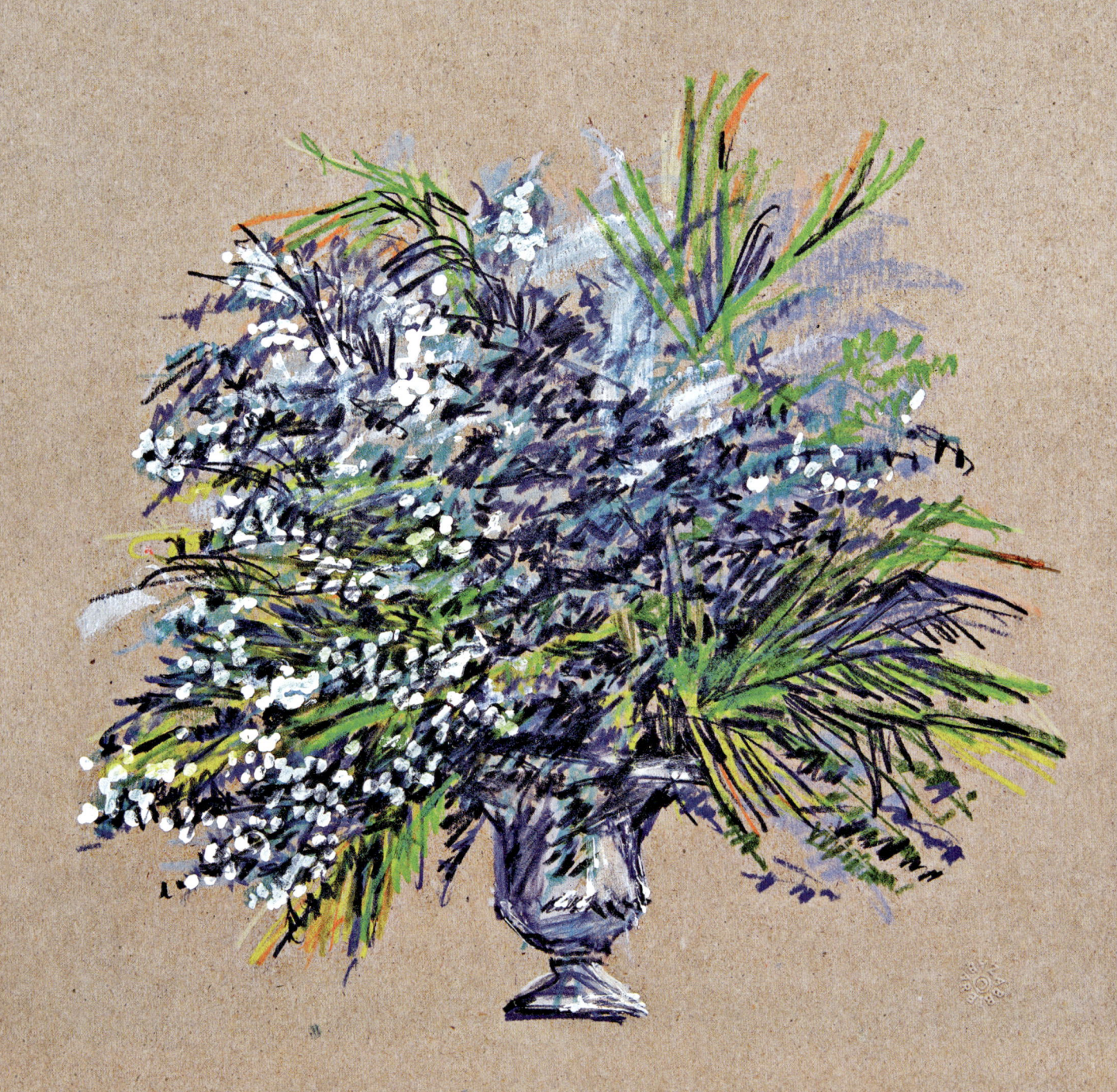

22 September:

Just *Eucalyptus* leaves and palm fronds. After the World Trade Center destruction, Chris said that there were no flowers in the market, just greens.

Colored pencil with whiteout on cardboard, 8 x 8¾ in

24 September:

I consider this one of my seminal works. It was the first drawing I did on cardboard. I was so excited I forgot to write any notes about what the bouquet was made of.

Colored pencil and whiteout on a piece of cardboard
from the Chinese laundry, 7¼ x 7¼ in

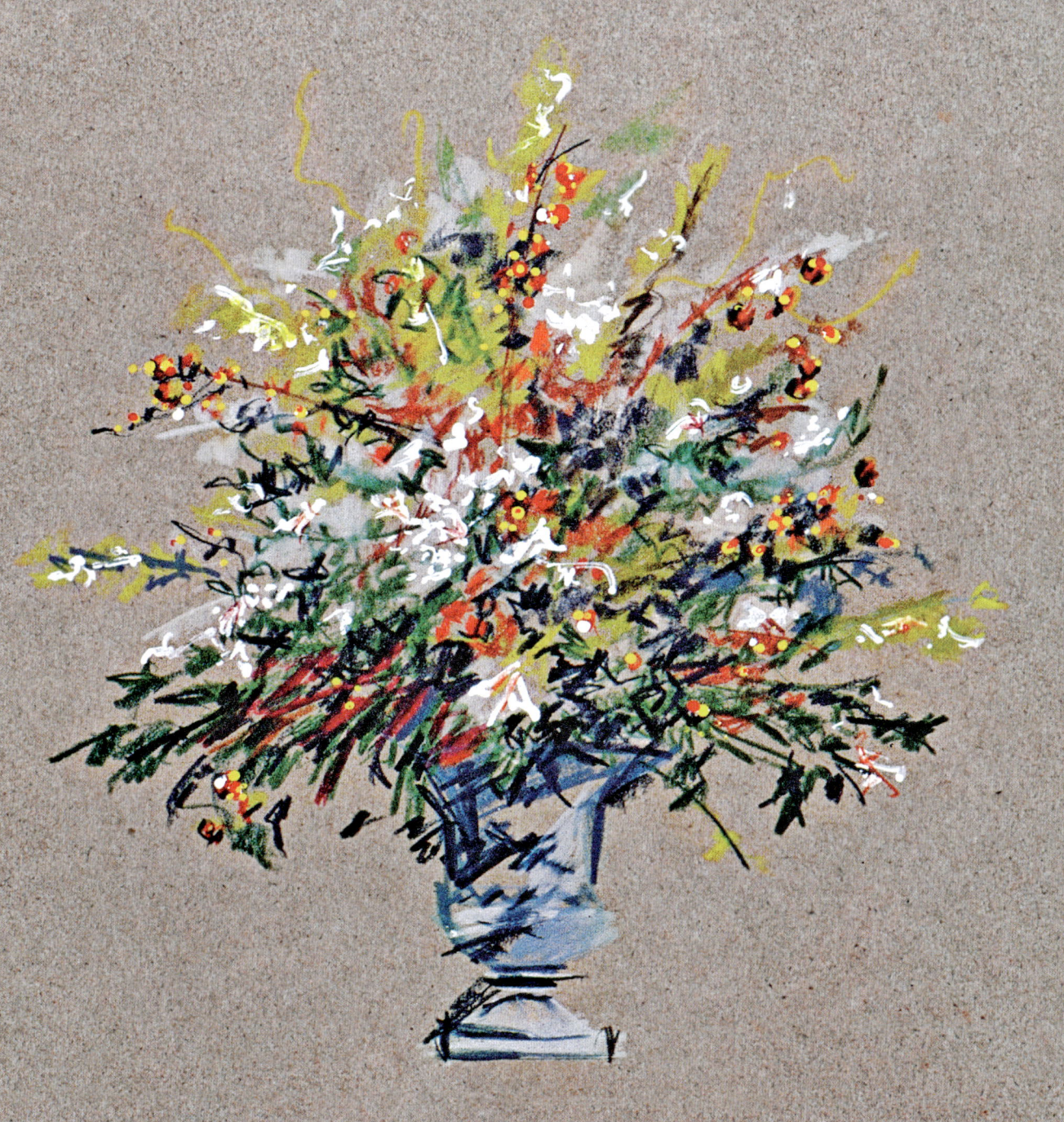

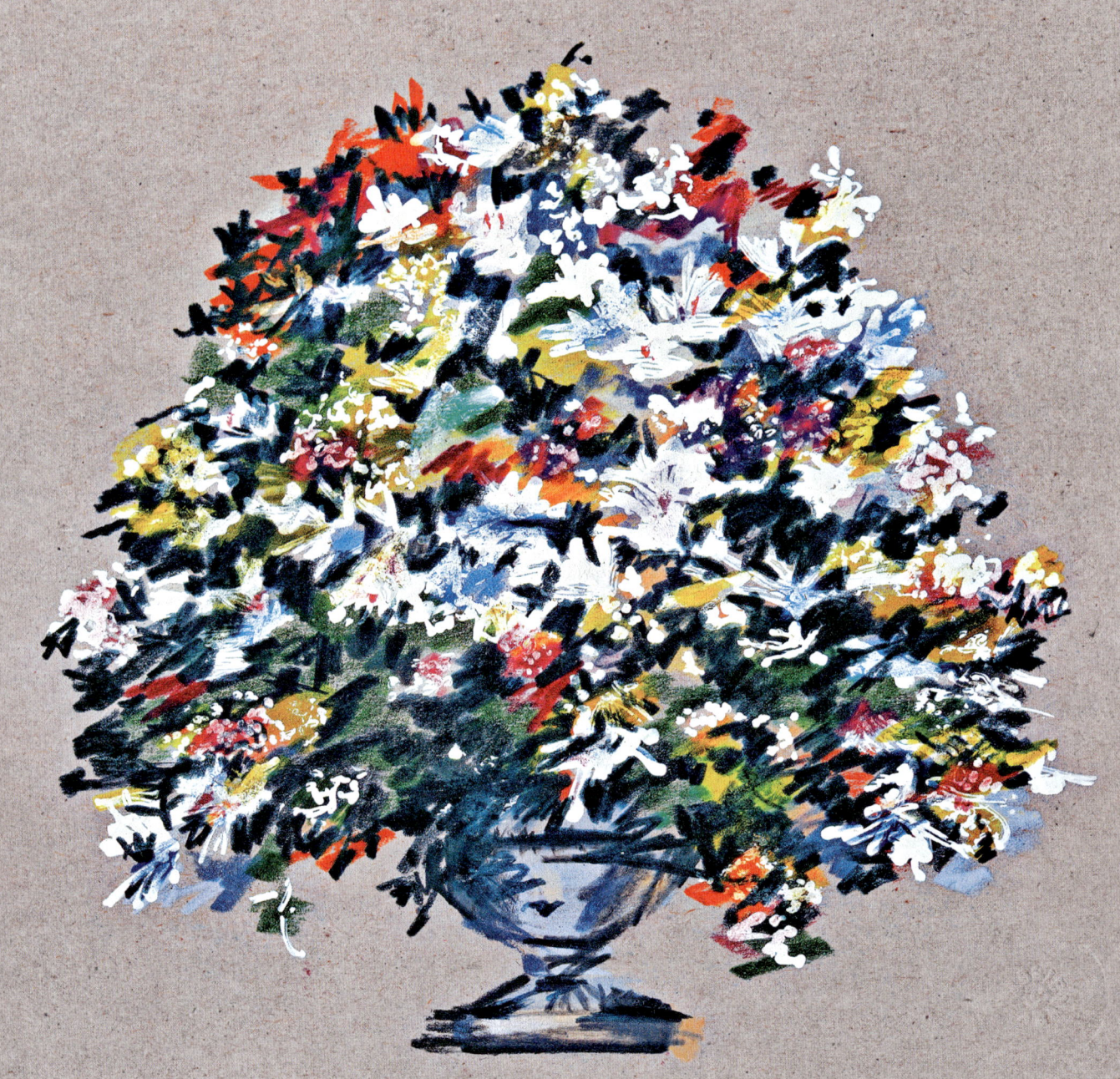

24 September:

Hydrangeas, lilies and magnolia leaves.

Colored pencil and whiteout on cardboard, 7½ x 7¾ in

30 September:

Eucalyptus, palm leaves and lilies.

Colored pencil and whiteout on cardboard, 7⅞ x 7⅜ in

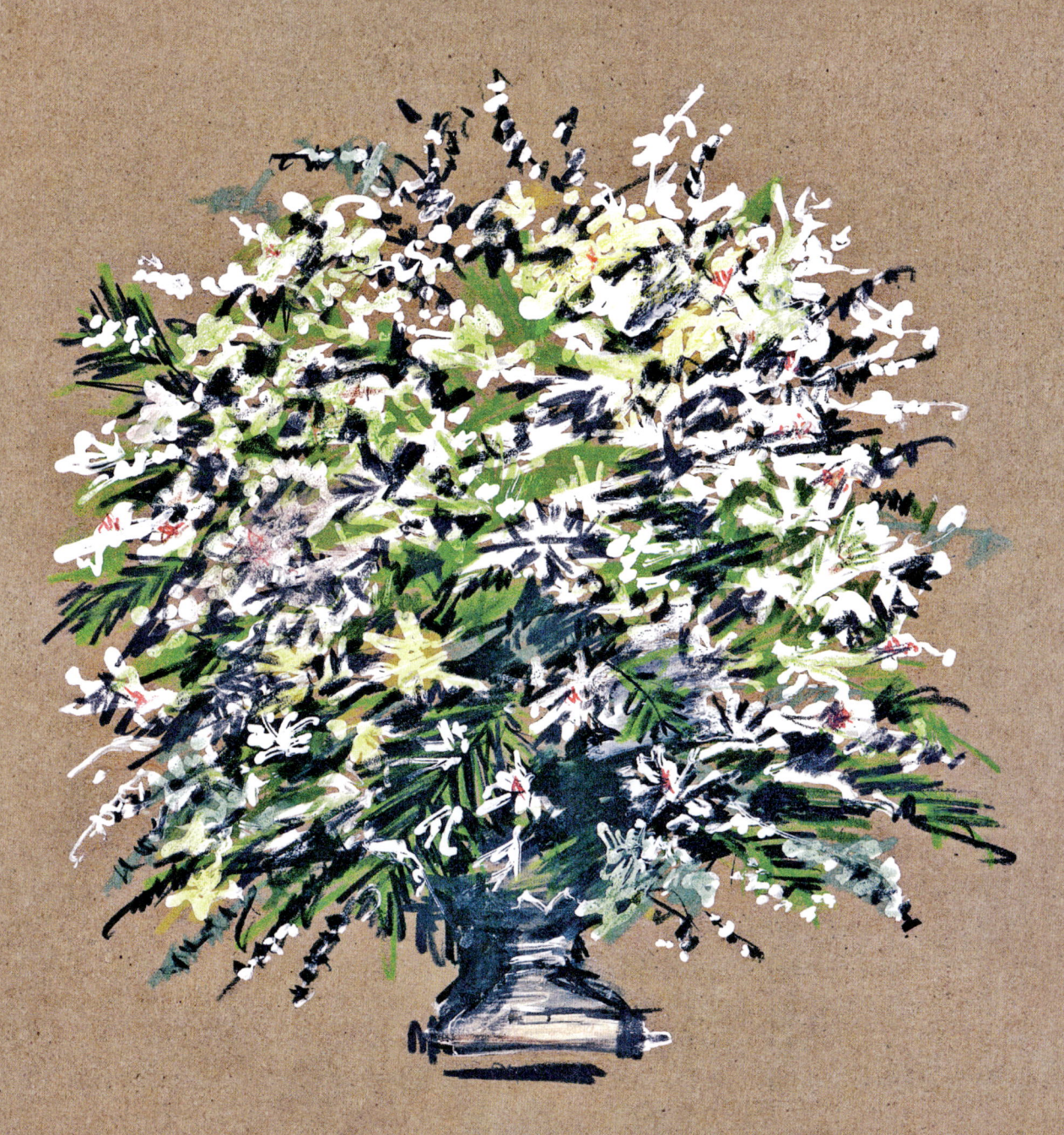

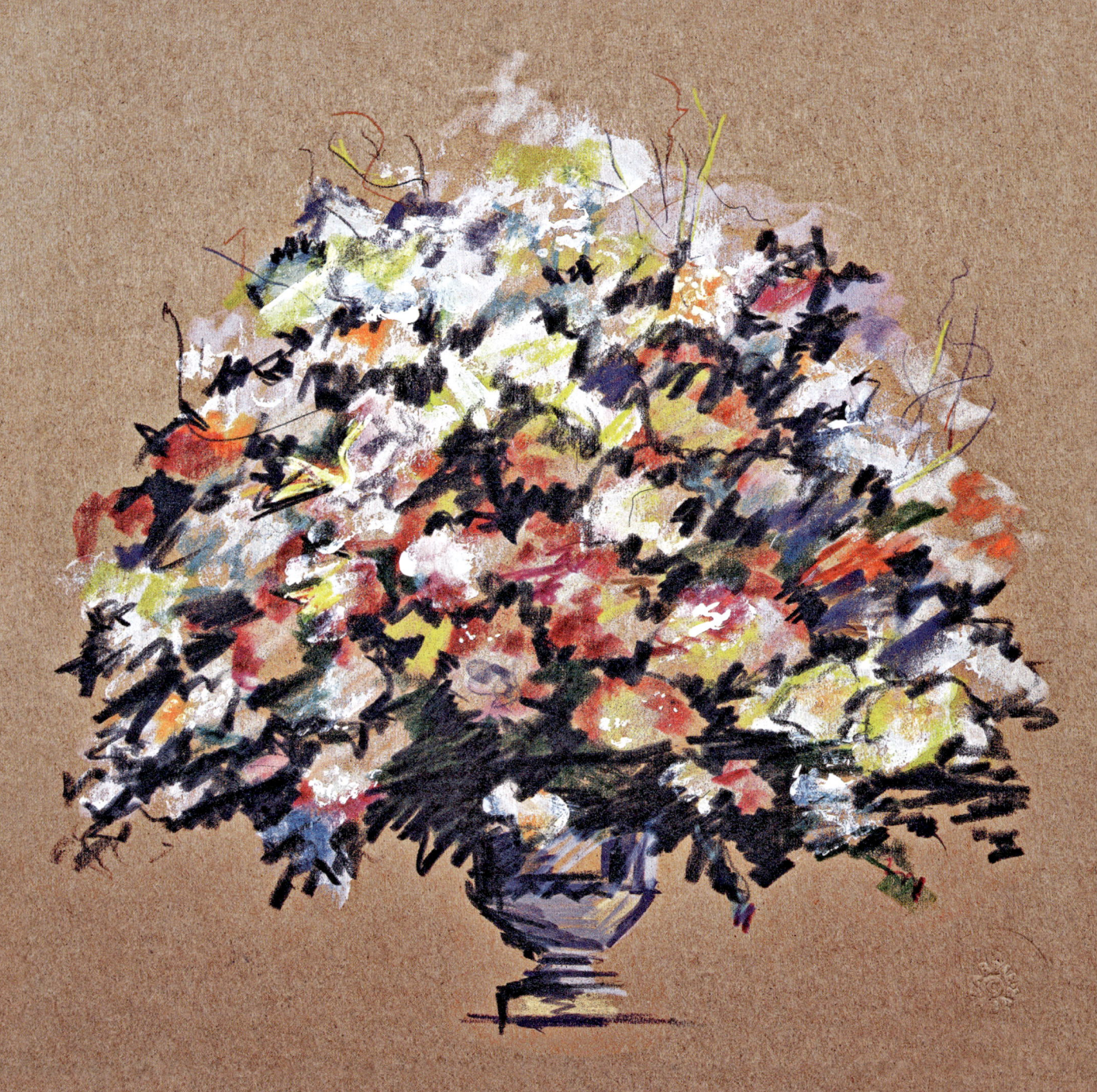

7 October:

A few lilies, but otherwise all hydrangeas in the process of a beautiful death. I just came crosstown from visiting my mother, who is also at the end of her life. Always troubling—no lights are on when I arrive at the museum. I turn around and start walking out. The guard says, "So soon?" He flips a few switches. Suddenly, I feel less troubled.

I also felt like I had to stay and draw this arrangement. More for him, than for me.

Colored pencil and whiteout on cardboard, 8¼ x 8¼ in

9 October:

Lots of greens and some lilies.

Colored pencil on cardboard, 6¾ x 7⅛ in

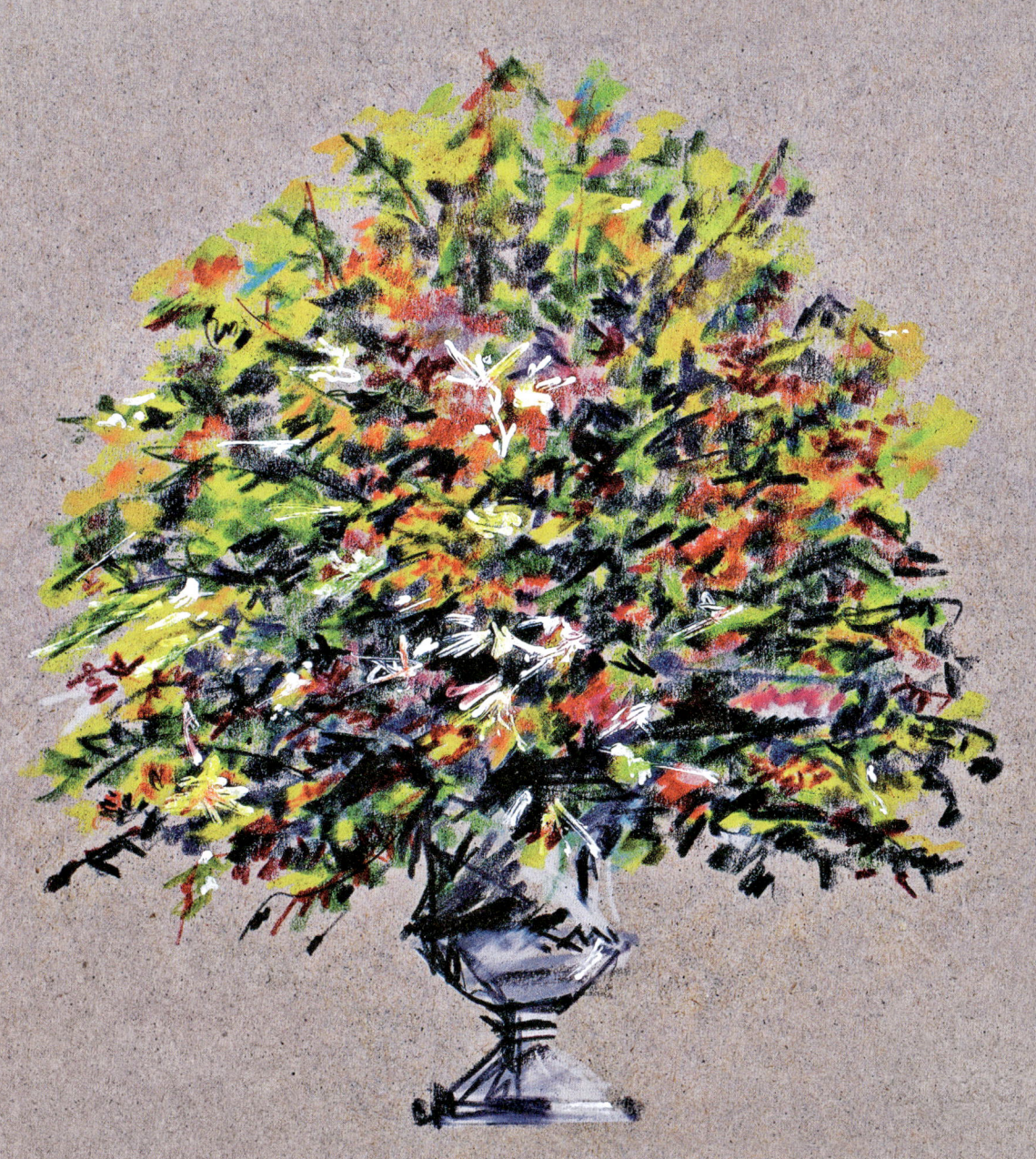

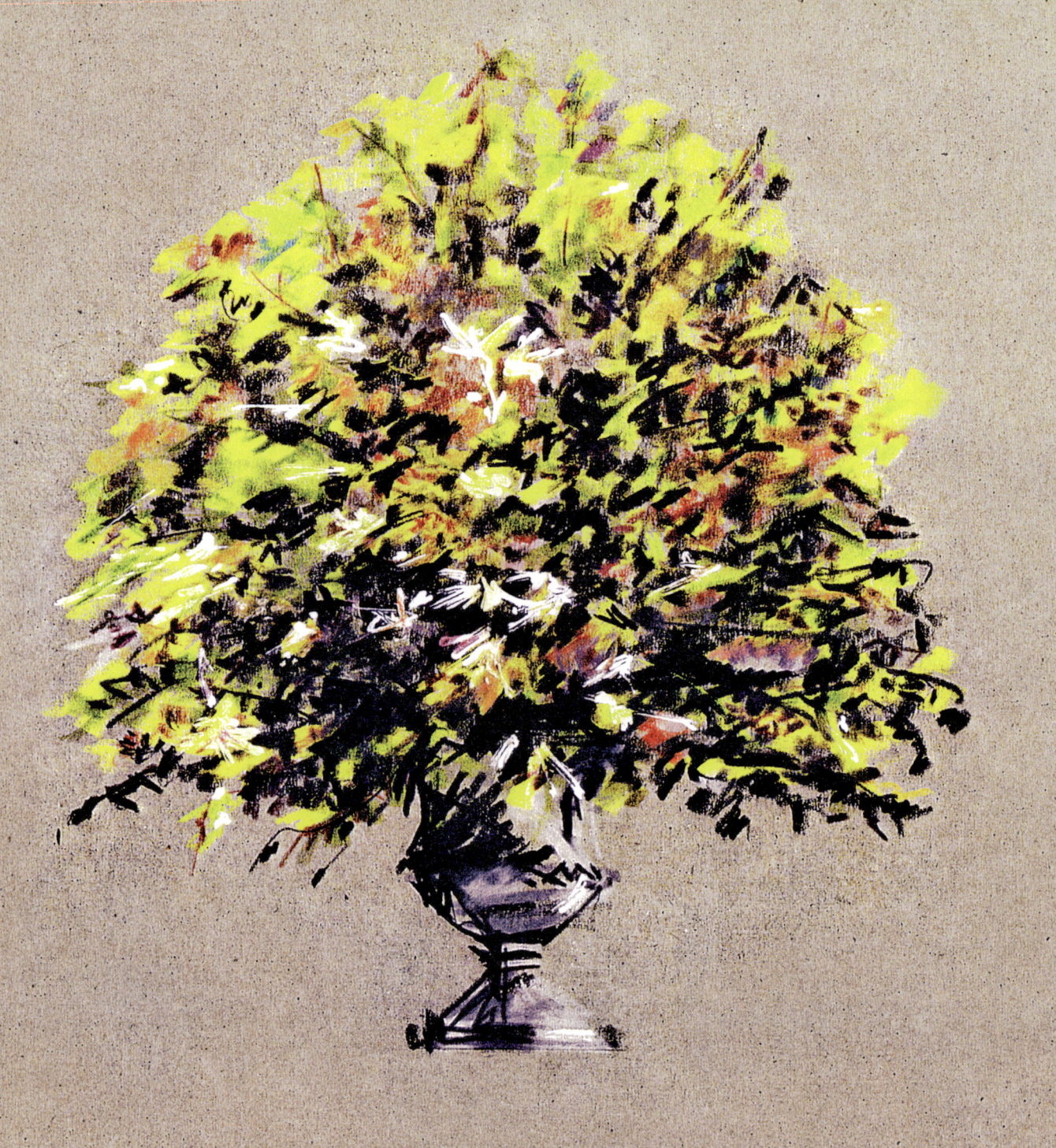

10 October:

Colored pencil on cardboard, 6¾ x 7¼ in

14 October:

First profusion of seasonal bittersweet berries. Big, bushy, dried-up hydrangeas, brown oak leaves on some branches and evergreen leaves on others.

Colored pencil with lots of whiteout on cardboard and I added red and yellow stippled enamel berries when I got back home, 8⅜ x 8½ in

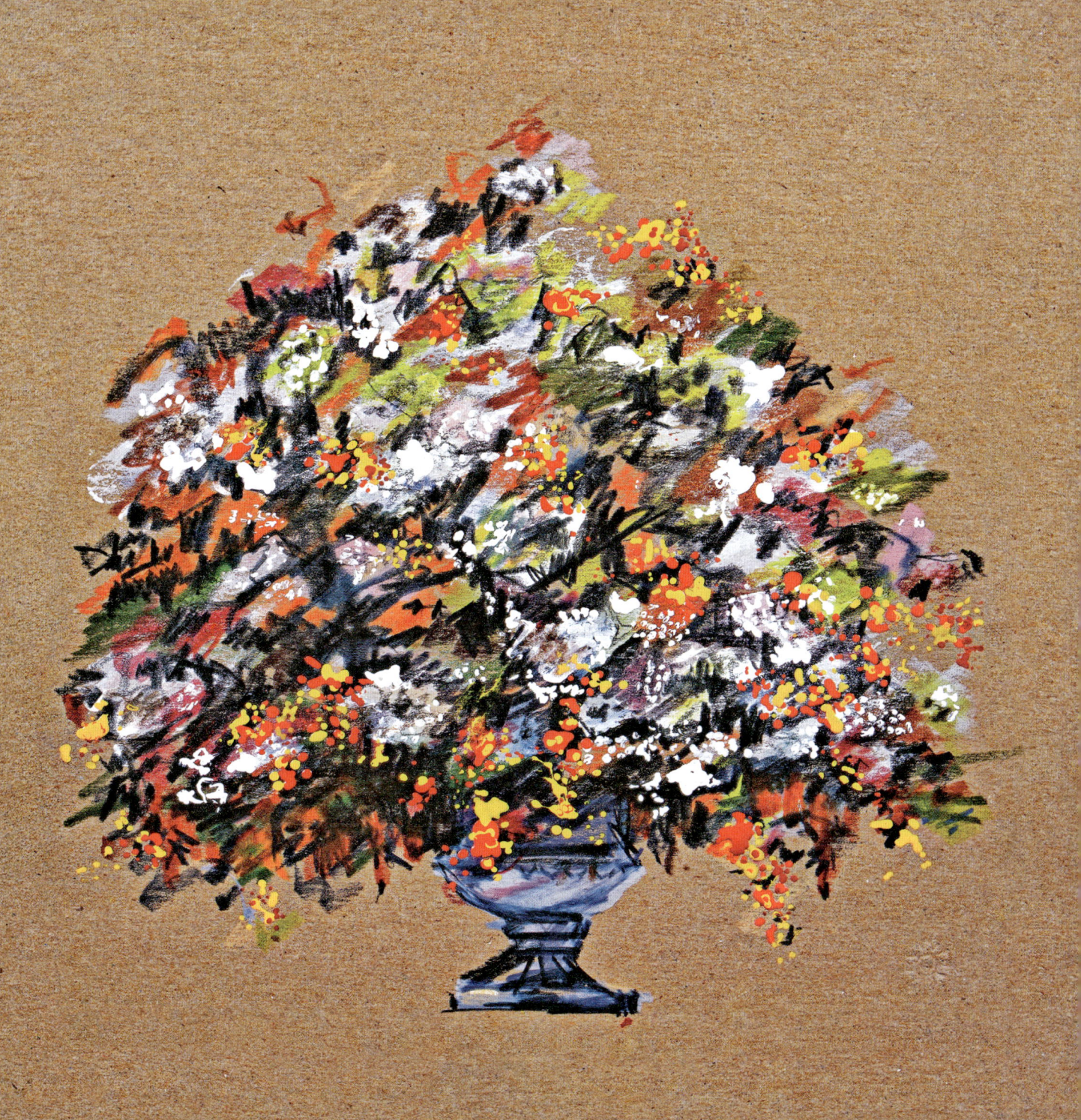

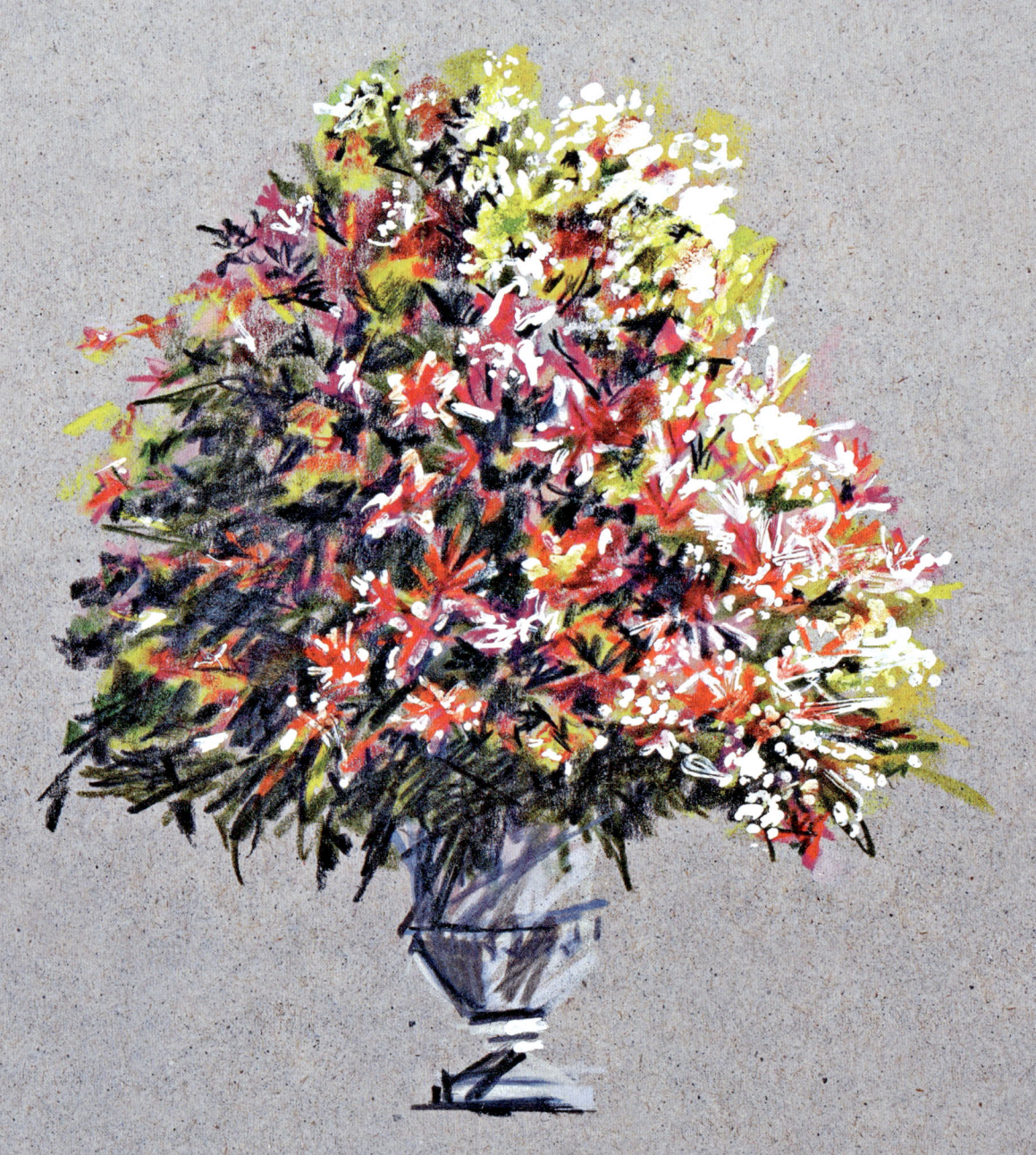

16 October:

Loads of lilies. Terrific chiaroscuro light.

Colored pencil and whiteout on cardboard, 6⅜ x 6⅞ in

21 October:

Hydrangeas, yellow- and apricot-colored lilies; autumn leaves but no maple leaves.
The guard turned on the lights for me again, so I stayed and drew the bouquet.

Colored pencil with smudged whiteout on cardboard, 8 x 8 in

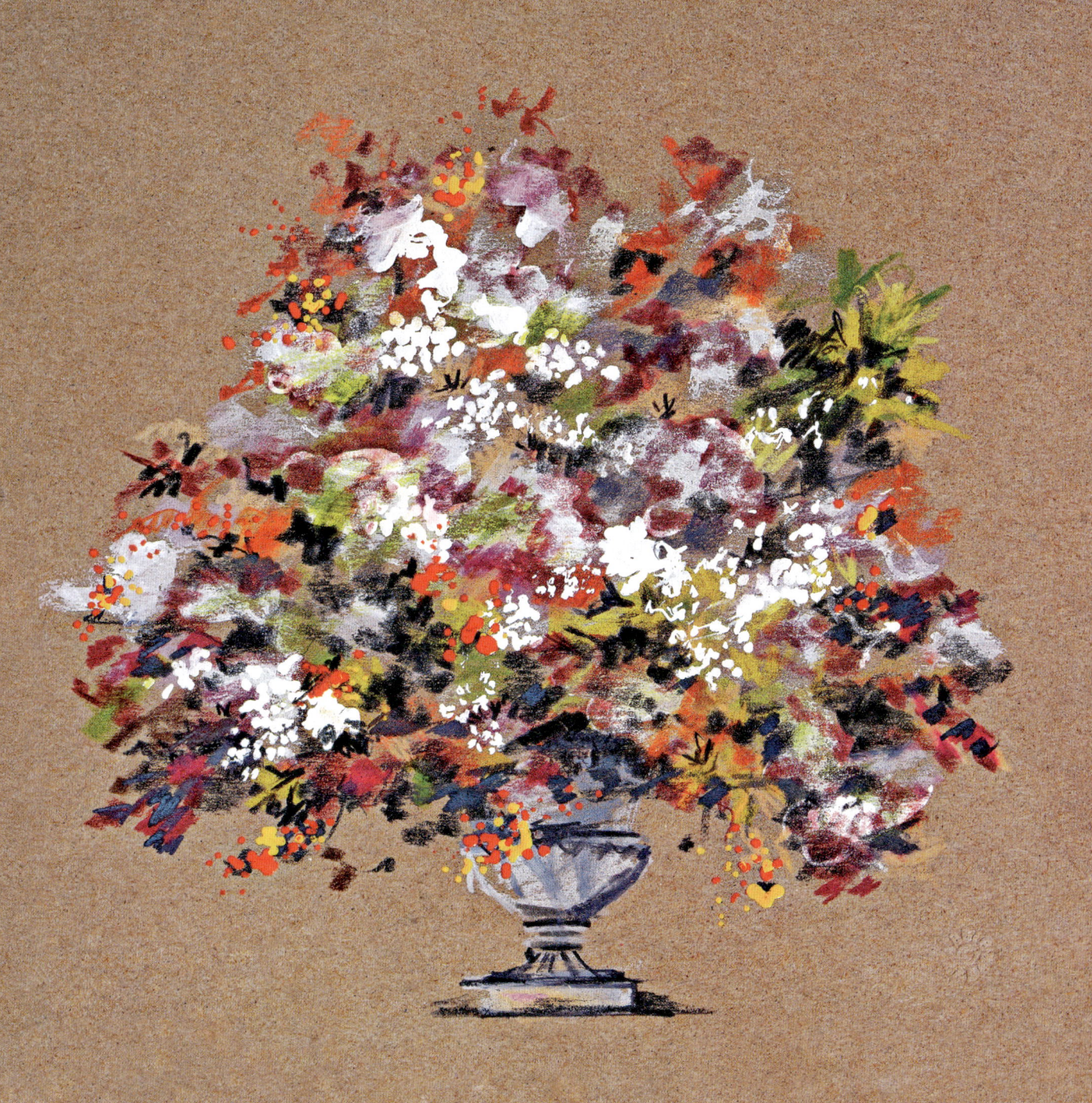

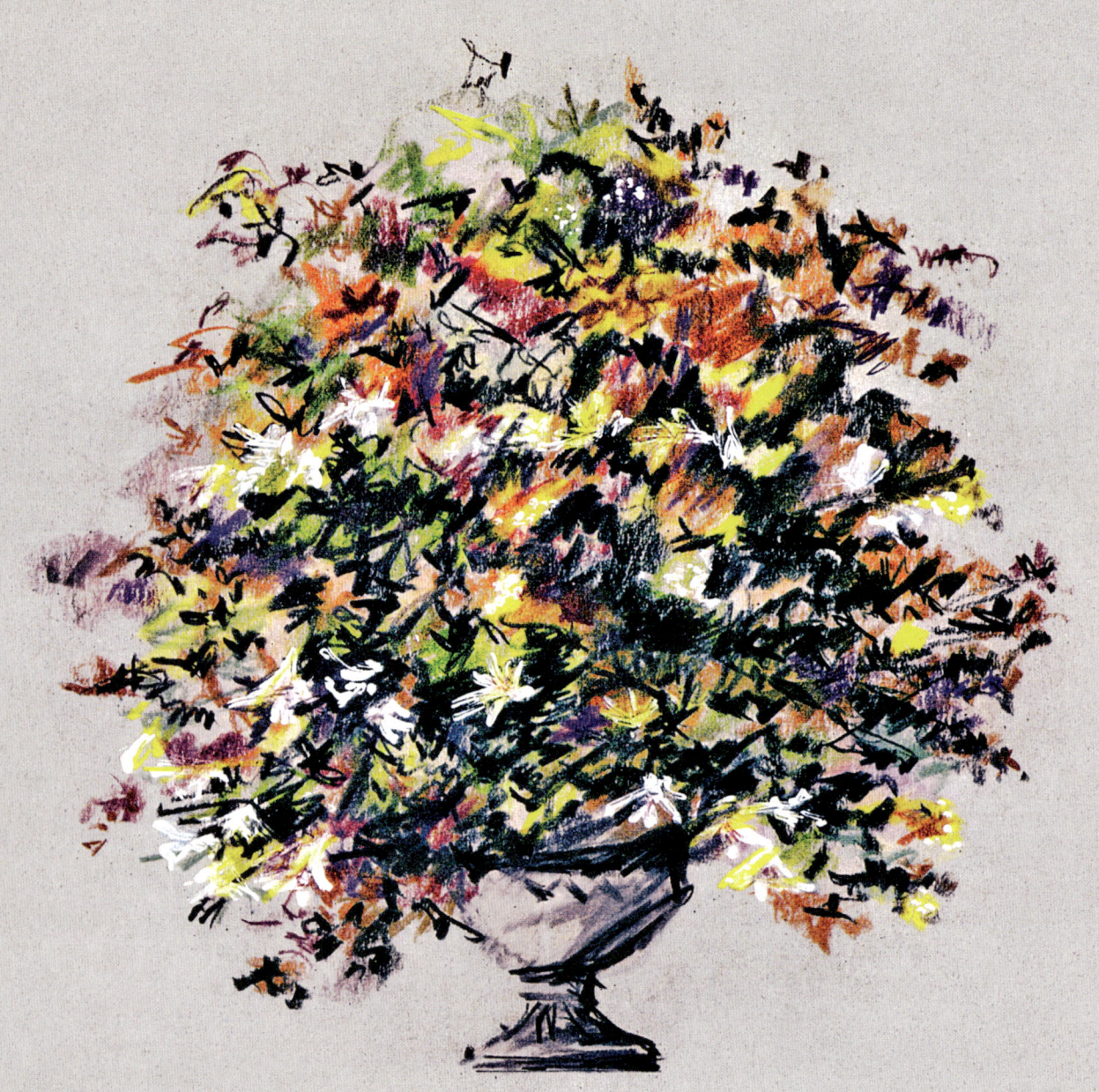

24 October:

I did this drawing of mostly autumn foliage on my birthday. It was bought by someone because it was also her birthday. It always fascinates me to know how people make their decisions.

Colored pencil on cardboard, 7 x 7 in

30 October:

Autumnal bouquet with lots of local roadside materials: berries, evergreens, branches of native oak leaves, soft junipers that do not turn color when they dry up.

Enamel and colored pencil on cardboard, 6⅝ x 7½ in

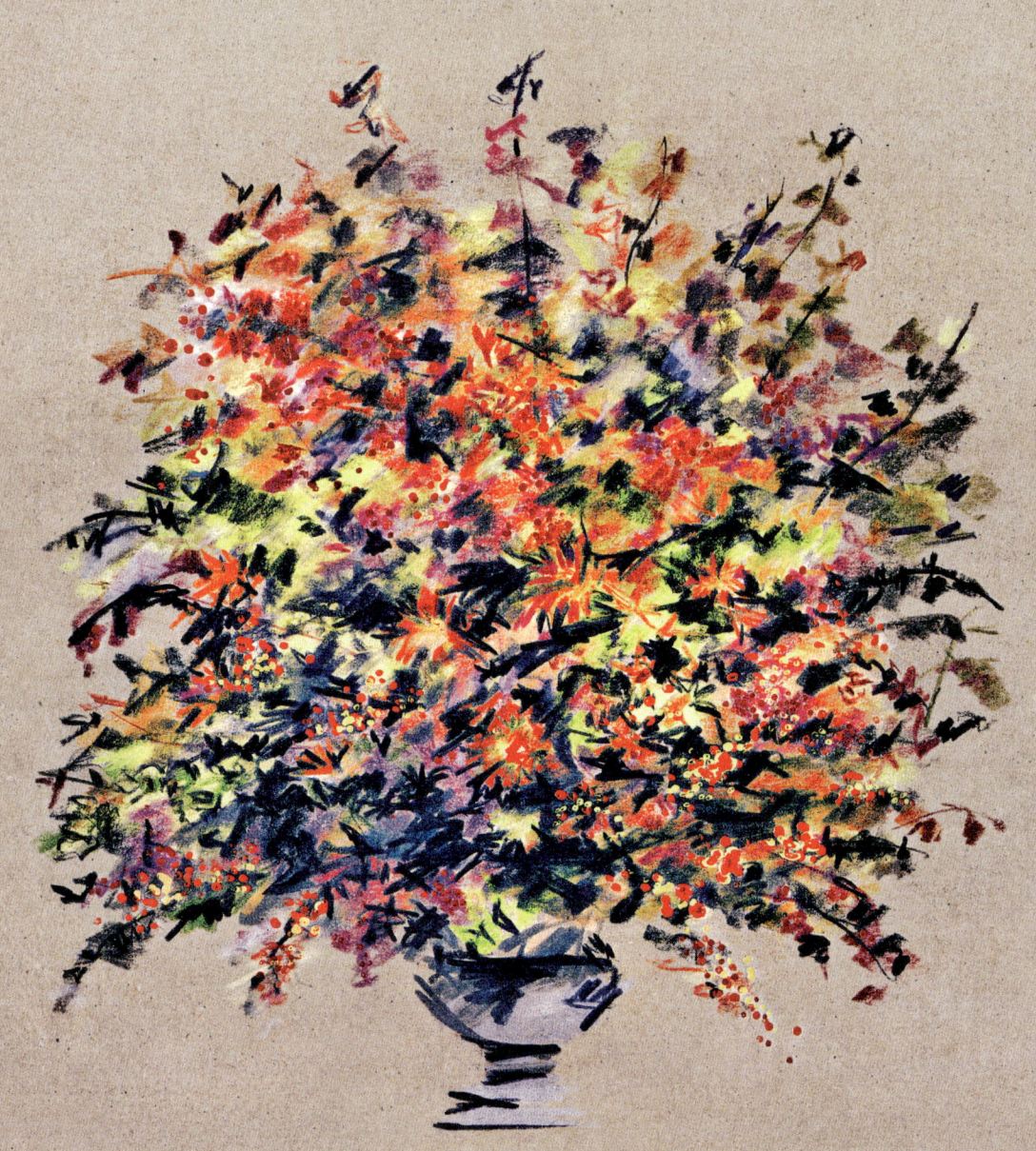

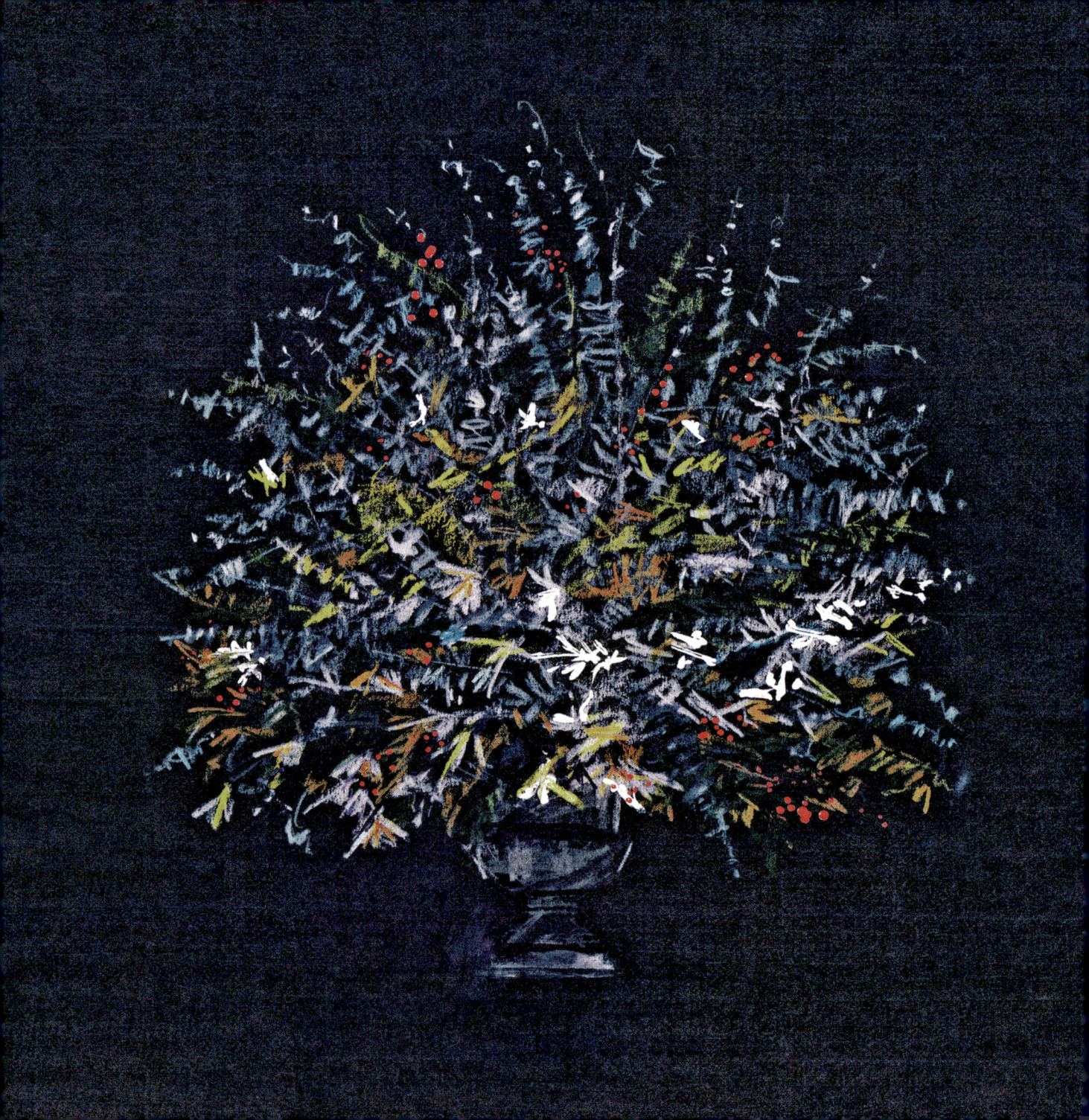

13 November:

Colored pencil on black paper, 6⅜ x 7 in

19 November:

With this bouquet, I gained a new appreciation for *Amaranthus caudatus*, also known as love-lies-bleeding, an annual flowering plant with drooping tassels of red or gold flowers that can grow up to 12 inches long.

Colored pencil and enamel on cardboard, 7½ x 7½ in

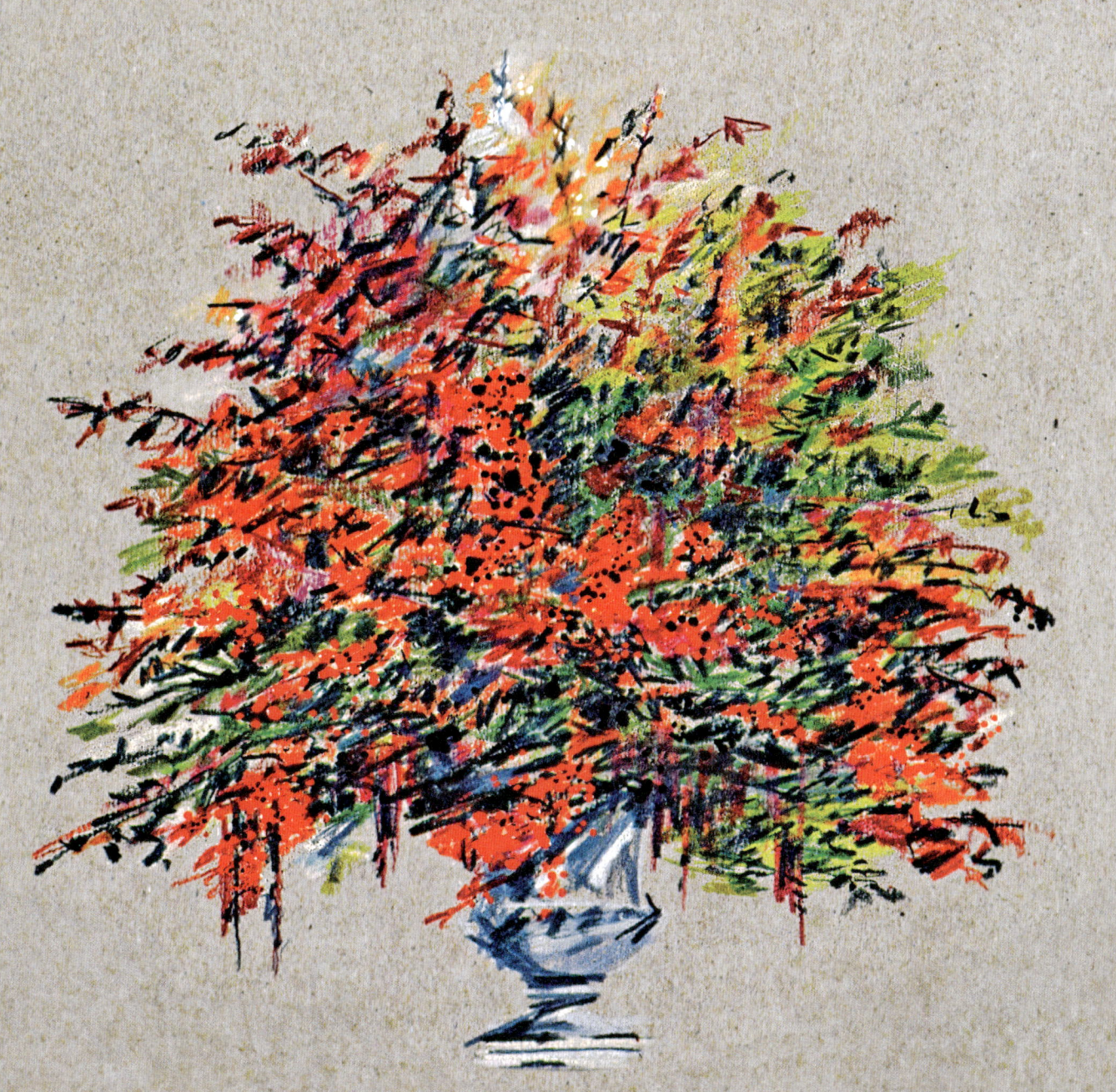

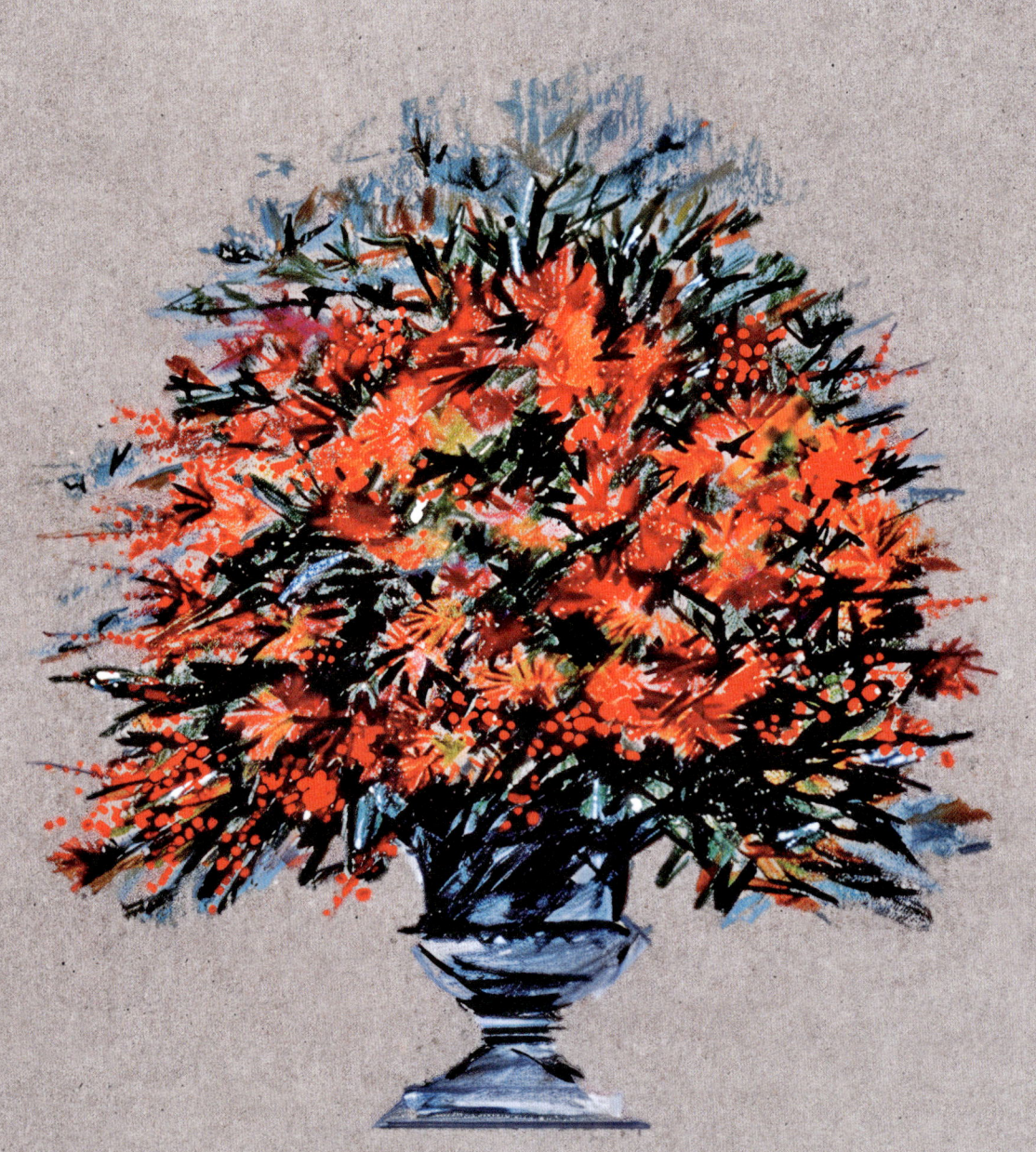

27–28 November:

Greens and seasonal berries.

Colored pencil on cardboard, 6⅞ x 7⅛ in

30 November:

Even on the gloomy morning of this holiday weekend, a polka-dotted bouquet—with red berries throughout—can make you smile. Plus, there are dahlias that have survived an early frost, but the dramatic poppies are fully opened already and might have to be replaced. After all, those big, red, horticultural marvels are front and center at Thanksgiving.

Colored pencil on paper, 7 x 7¼ in

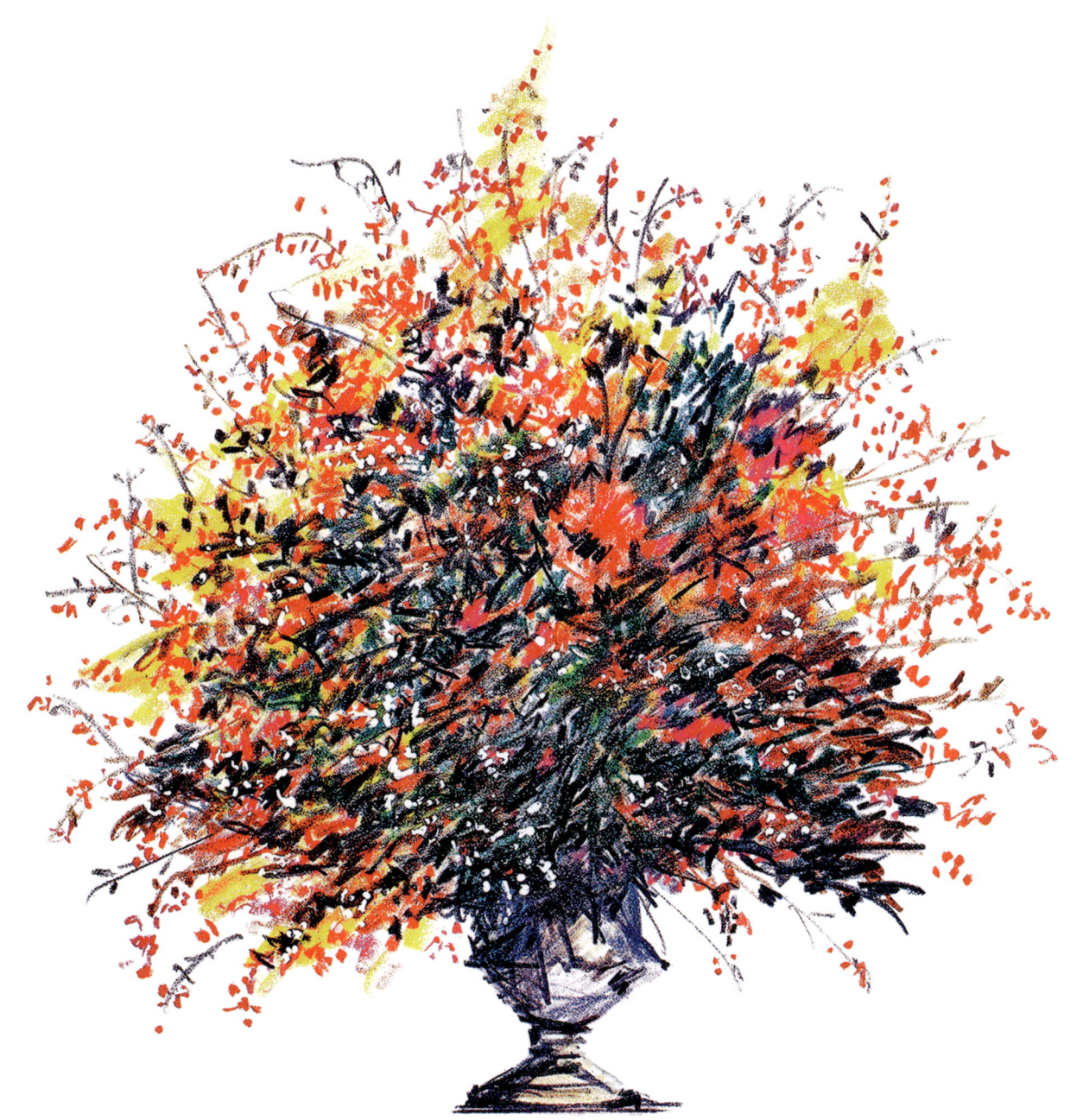

Winter

In late Winter, the most breathtaking bouquets had forced branches of a single theme. The dramatic brilliance of snow-white quince, golden yellow forsythia, and pink apple blossoms foretold the coming months in the garden. Though branches with catkins of pussy willows came right before the magnolia flowers, in the meantime they were just furry fillers.

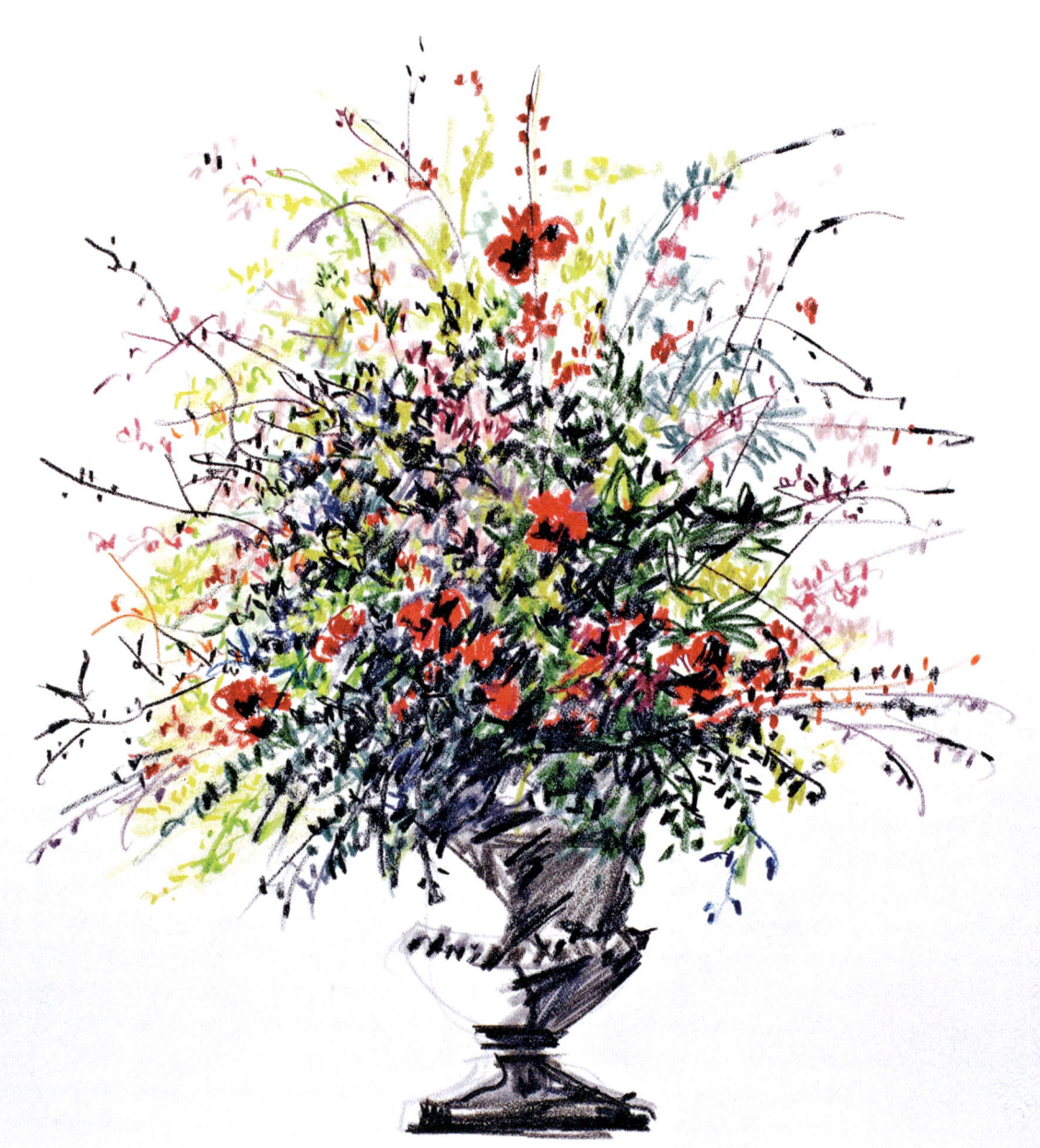

6 December:

It's 8:20 a.m. and it feels like everyone is still asleep after last night's Costume Institute Gala. A totally uninhibited Christmas bouquet with thick-cut stalks of red amaryllis, forced quince branches, white lilies, white lilacs, pink spirea, *Eucalyptus*, winterberry branches and sprays of euphorbias.

Colored pencil on white rag paper, 8½ x 8½ in

7 December:

Magnolia leaves and fragrant lilies.

Colored pencil and whiteout on cardboard, 7⅜ x 8½ in

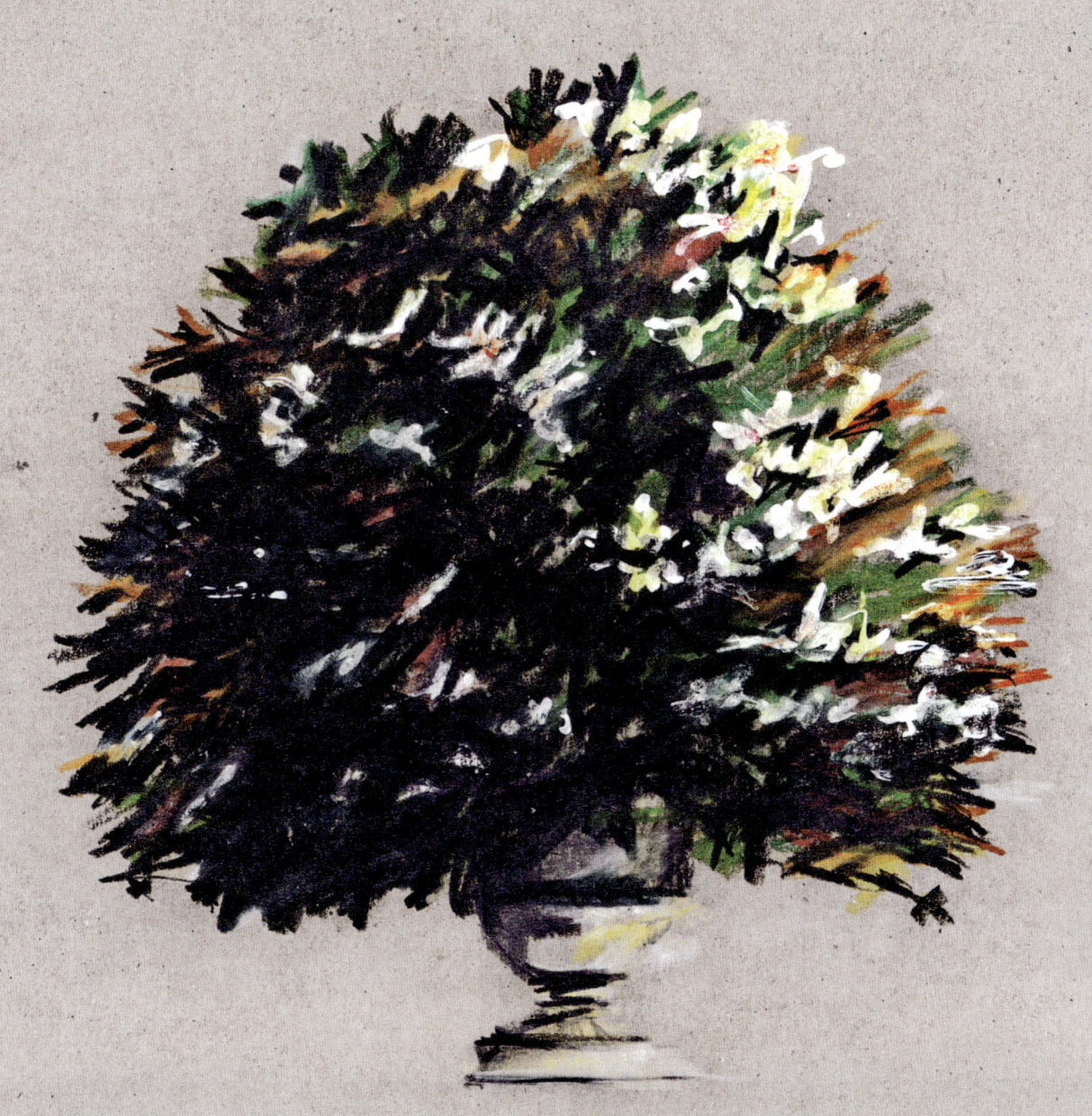

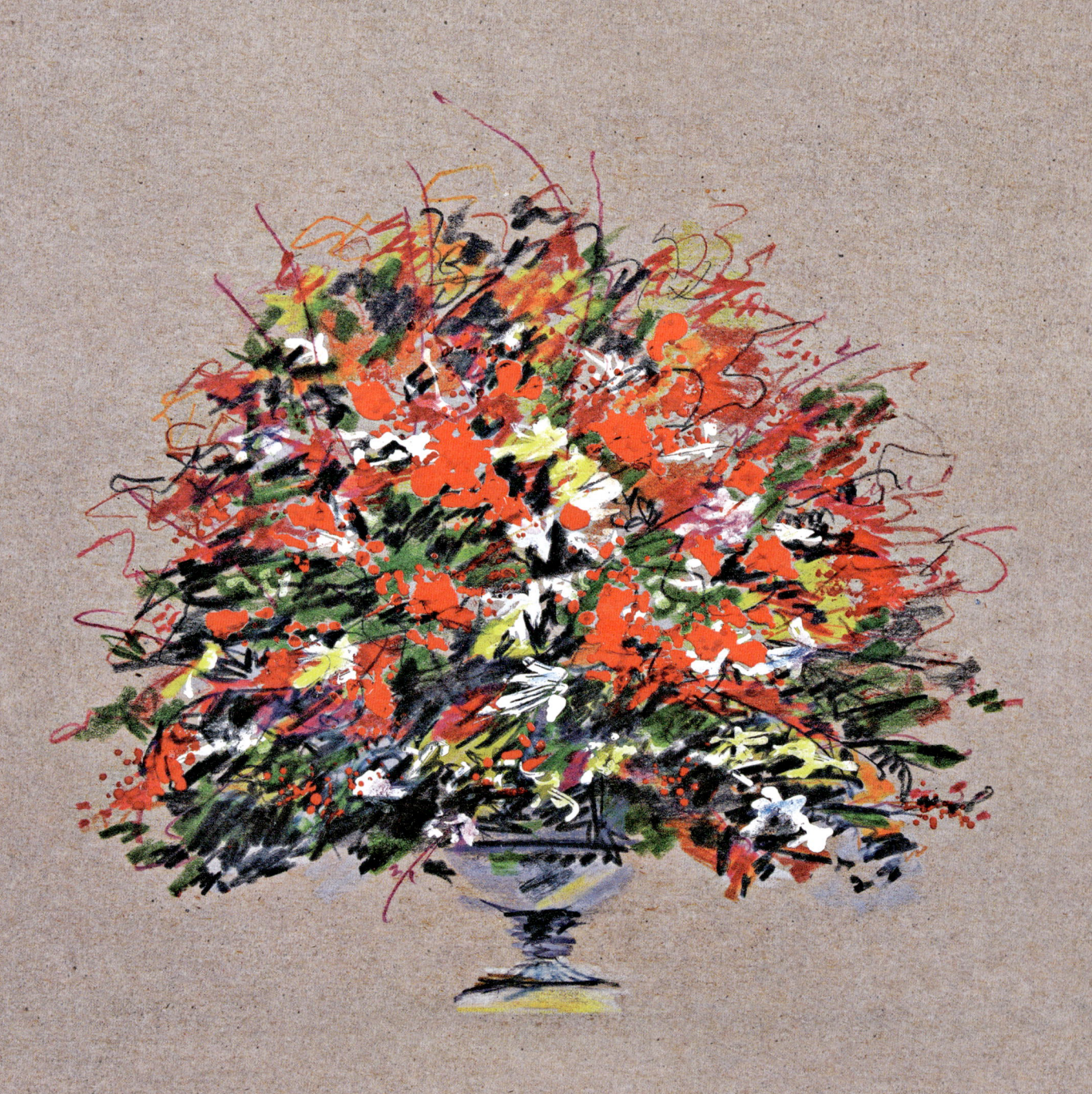

17 & 23 December:

A luscious holiday arrangement with shiny dark-green leaves of *Magnolia grandiflora*, as well as white lilies, red berries and lots of flyaway burgundy-colored branches. It started snowing heavily while I was working. Got a plastic bag from the gift shop and went home in a blizzard. I returned very early on Monday, hoping to finish. But Maintenance had already pulled the arrangement apart by 7 a.m.

Colored pencil, whiteout and enamel on cardboard, 8⅛ x 6¼ in

13 January:

Quince blossoms on branches, with *Eucalyptus* leaves, and pussywillow.

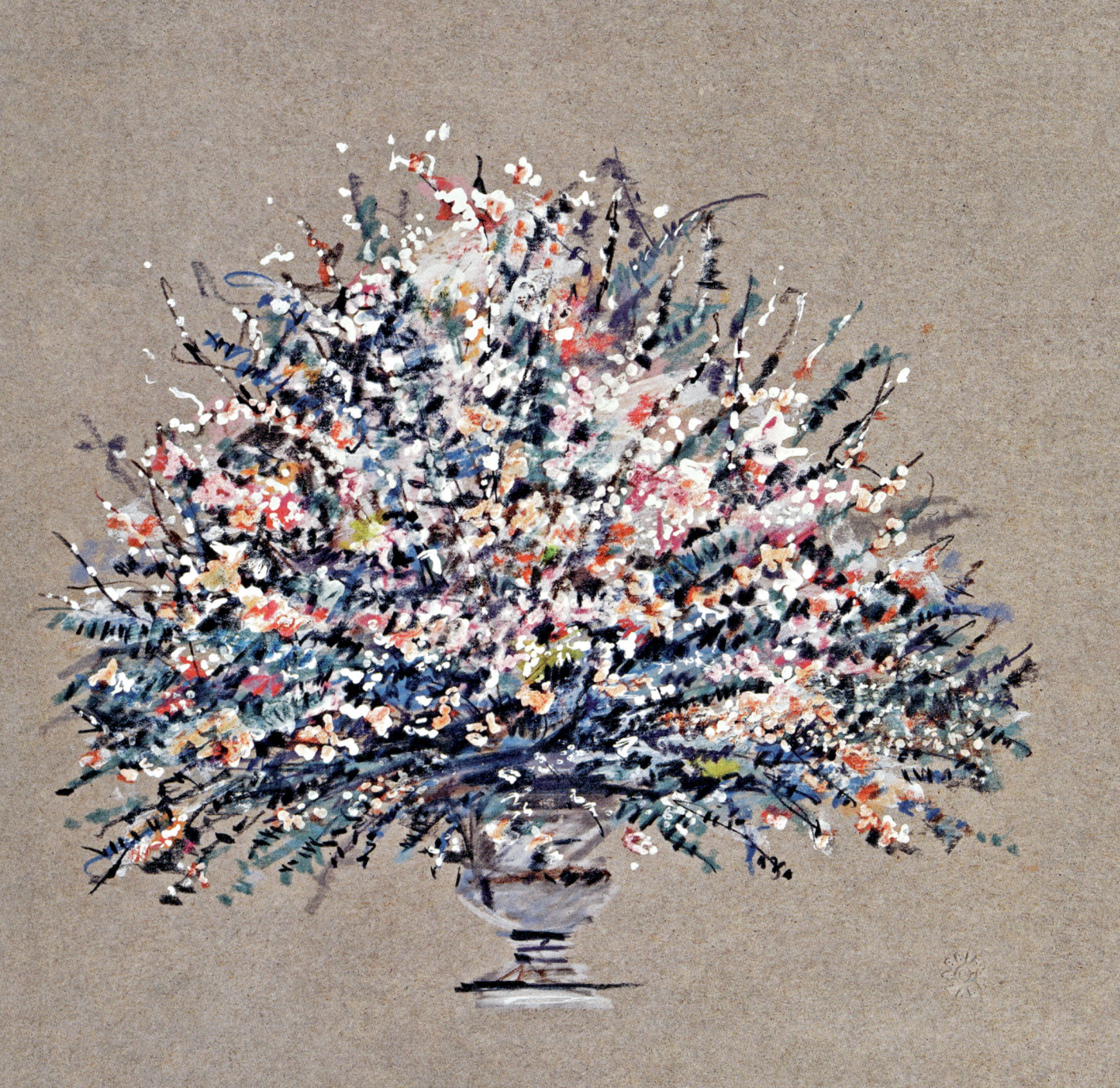

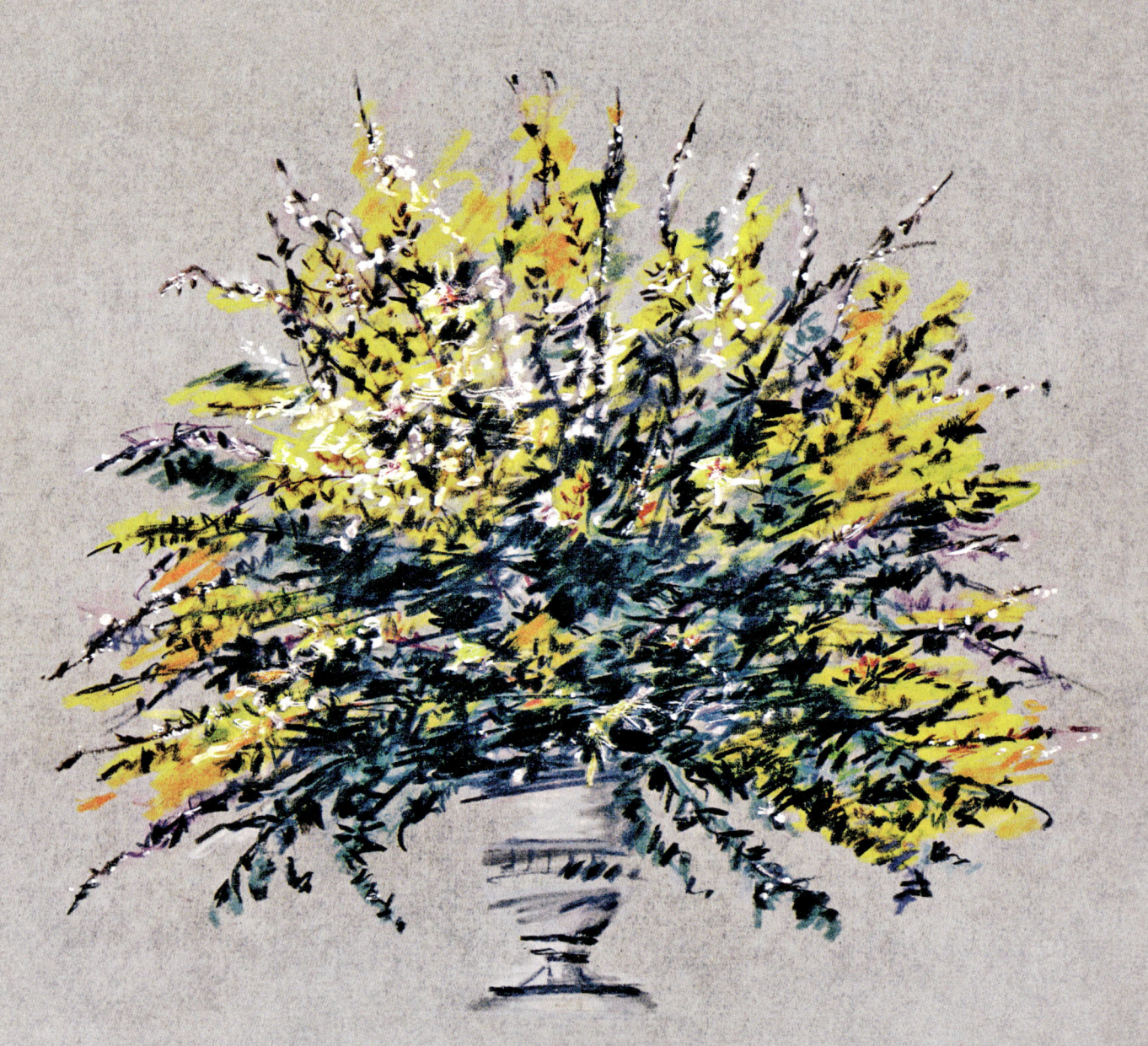

29 January:

Eucalyptus, lilies, beginning of forsythia branches, pussywillows not yet opened.

Colored pencil on cardboard, 7¼ x 8 in

1 February:

When I drew this arrangement for the first time, there were forced branches of quince and pussywillows. There were also palm fronds, white emperor tulips, some lilies and plump balls of unopened hydrangeas. The third time I returned to this drawing, it was because a friend had requested permission to reproduce this drawing on the cover of his privately published book about his wife who had recently died.

Initially drawn in 1997, it was reworked on 23 October 2002 and again, one last time, on 25 September 2024.

Colored pencil, red enamel, and whiteout on white rag paper, 8⅞ x 8⅜ in

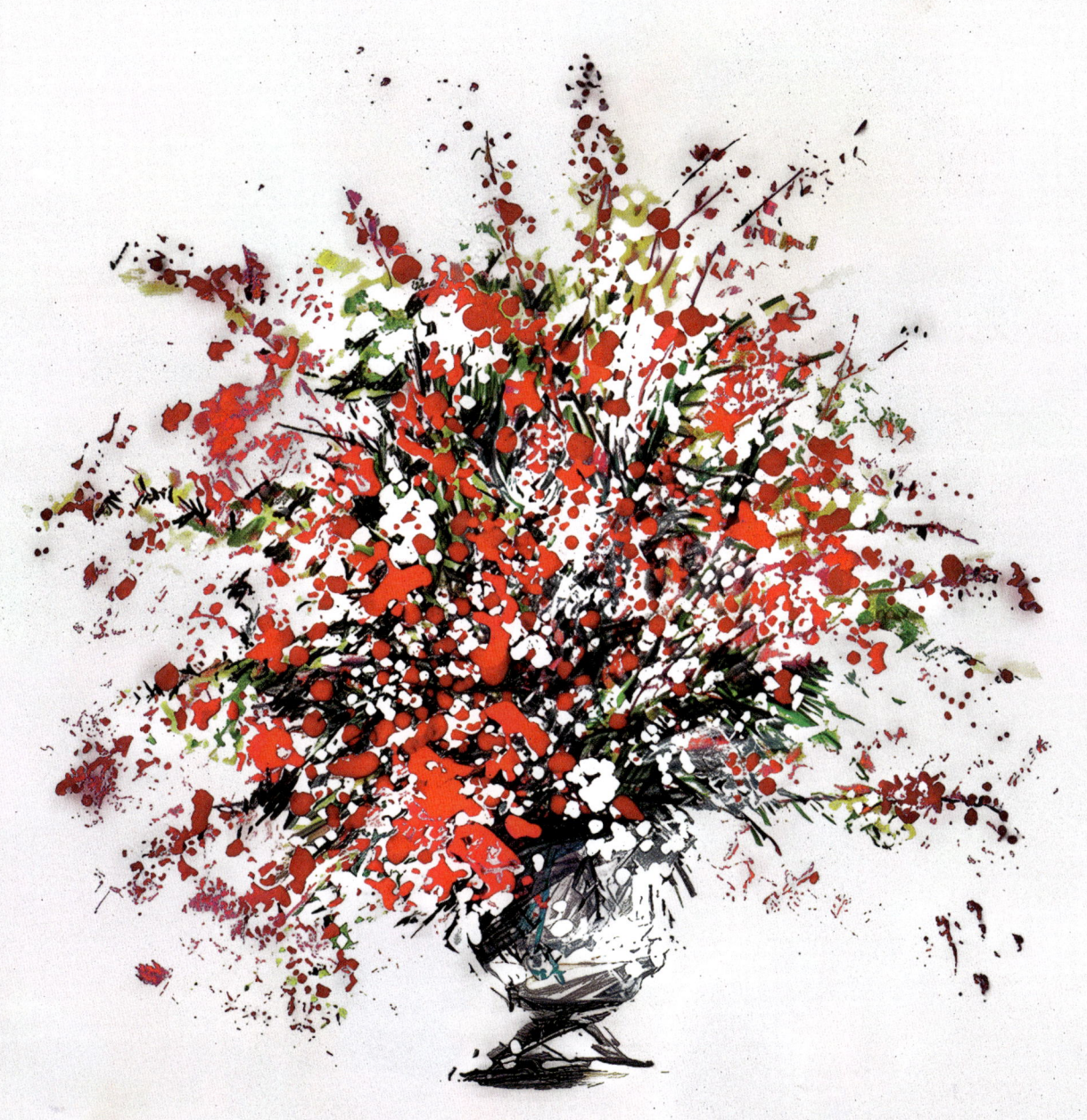

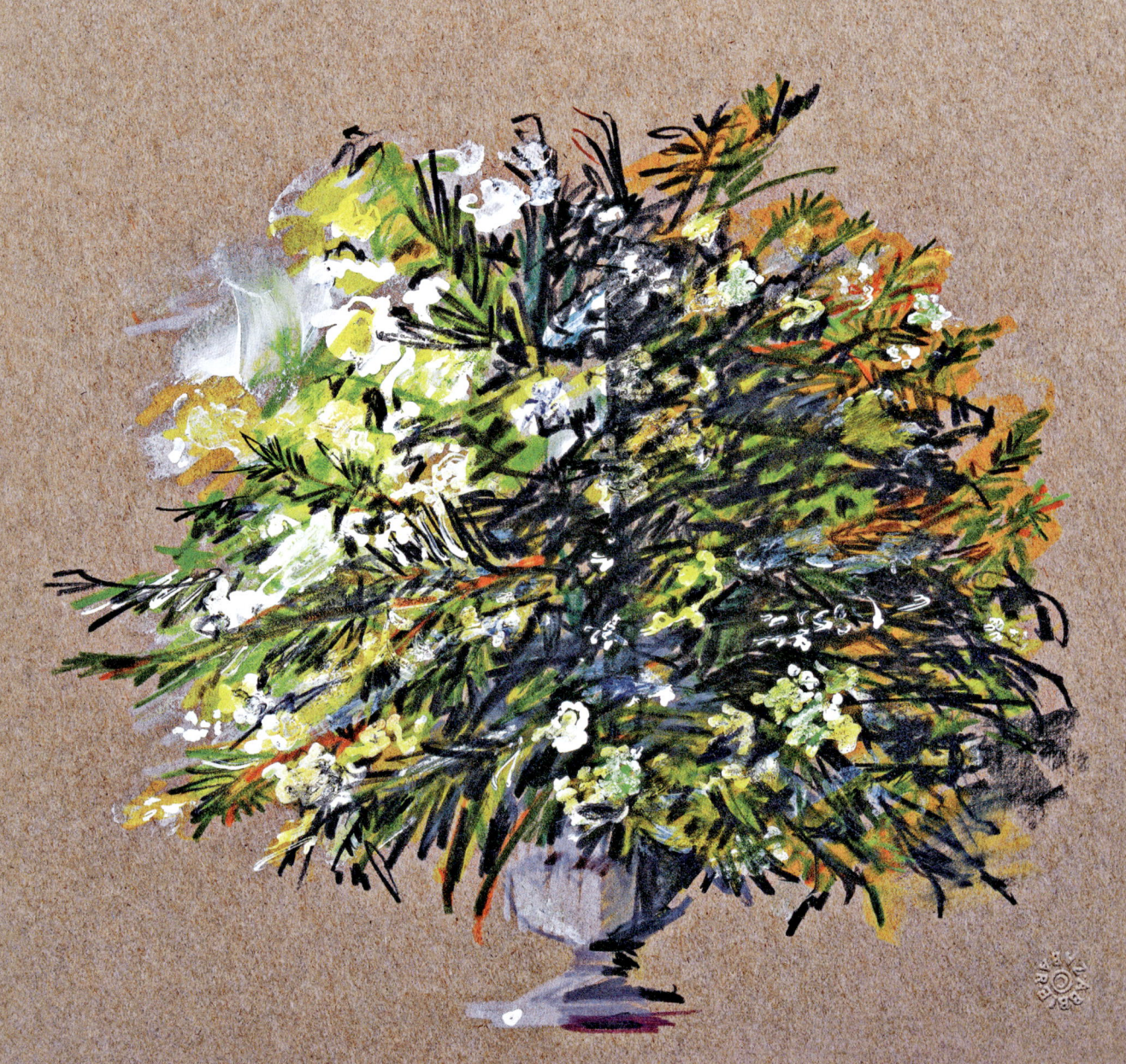

4 February:

A very monochromatic greenish-feeling bouquet with small flowers of *Hydrangea paniculata*, puff balls with lots of green and yellow foliage, variegated *Dracaena* leaves, and palm fronds. I loved doing this drawing, especially with that recurring challenge of the chiaroscuro light on the arrangement and the urn.

Rules seem to be getting tighter. That morning, the head of security wanted to know if the photo of the young woman who was fired yesterday had come down yet. Guards wanted to know why she was fired. So did I.

Colored pencil and whiteout on cardboard, 7¼ x 7½ in

The Blumenthal patio, originally belonging to the castle at
Vélez-Blanco, outside Almería, Spain. It was donated to the Met
Museum by George Blumenthal in 1941 and drawn by Abbie Zabar
in 2003.

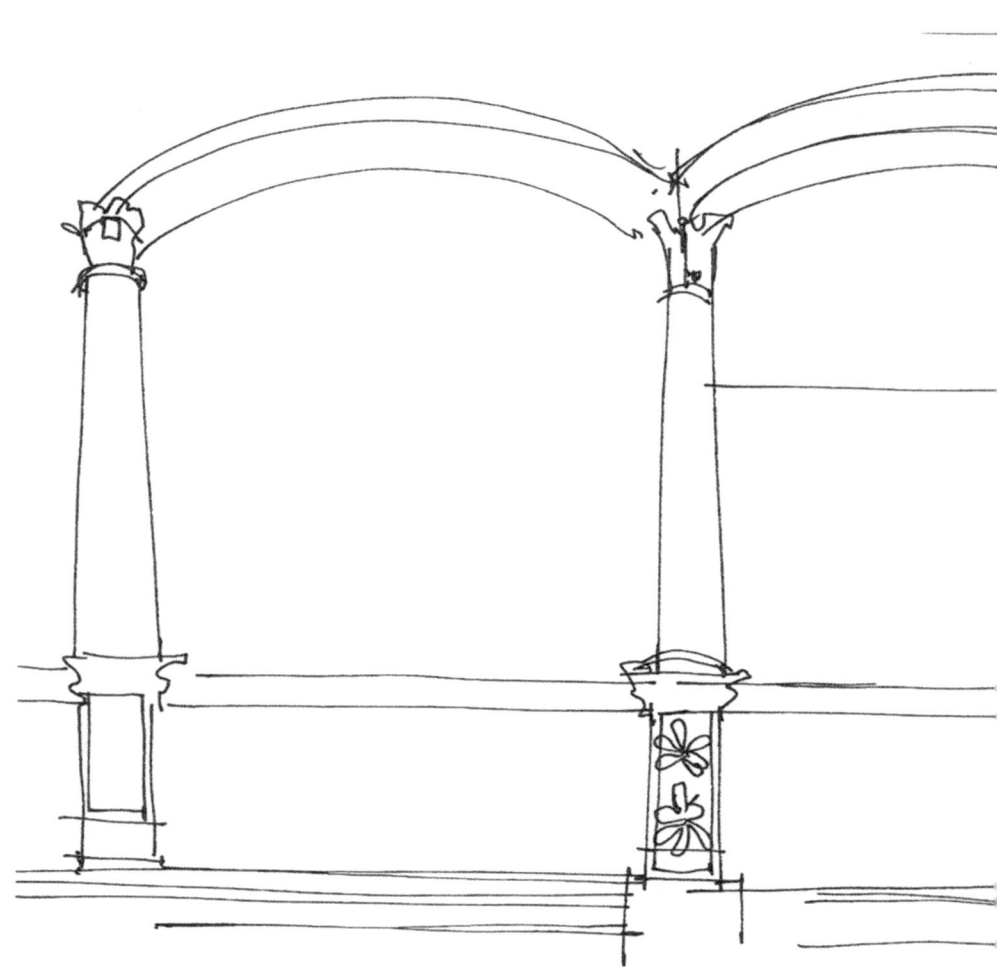

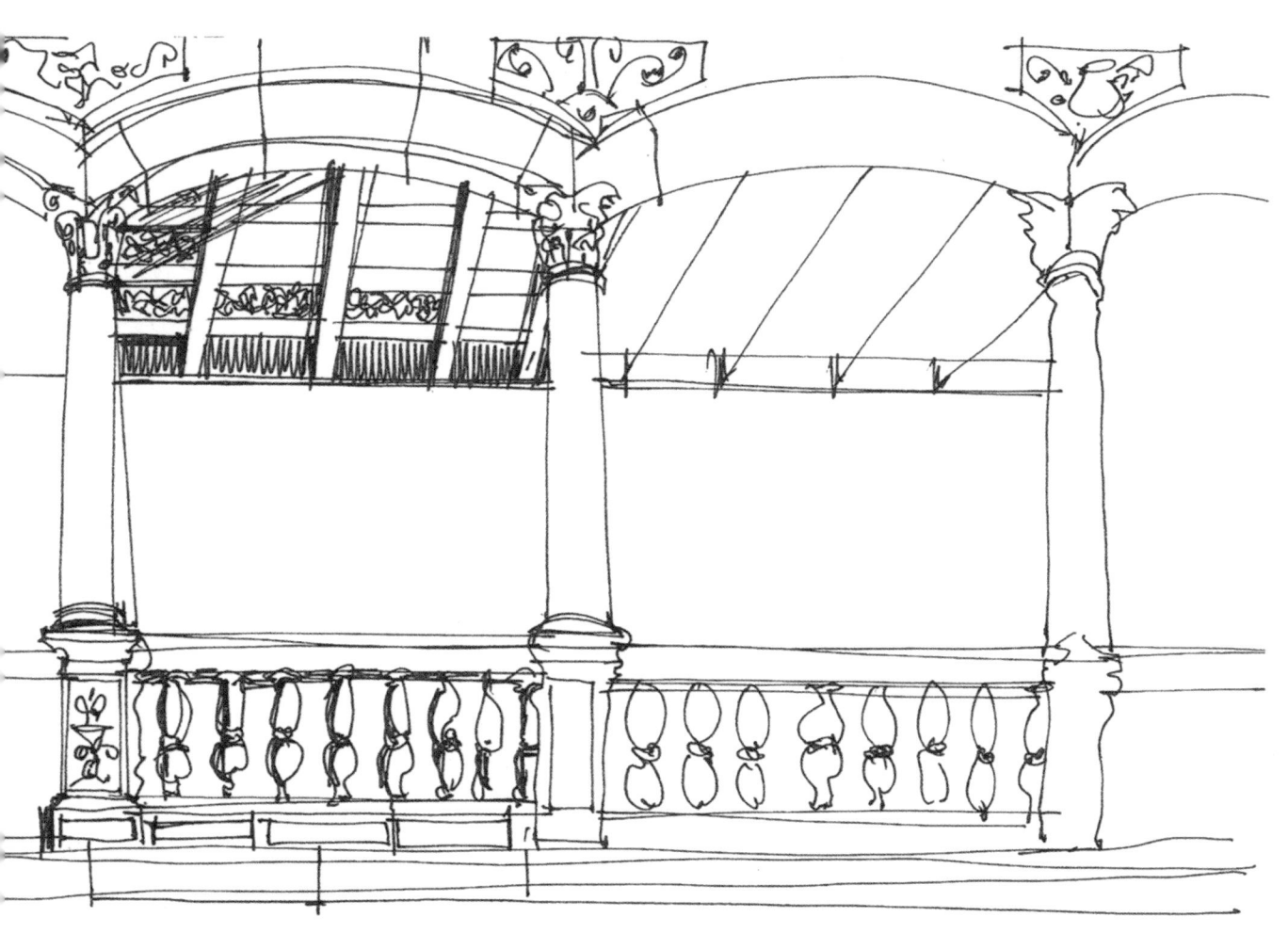

Afterword

Over the course of 10 years, the Department of Special Events renewed my contractual pass annually. No questions asked. The fingerprints and photo ID remained the same ones taken in 1994. With that laminated picture hanging around my neck, I had the luxury of entering the Great Hall before the Metropolitan Museum of Art opened to the public, solely to draw the bouquets. Imagine. It was as easy as taking a delivery up to a Carlyle guest suite, something else I took for granted.

But, after Tuesday 11 September 2001, all security tightened. They could only issue me a pass from month to month. I would need to check in on my flowers weekly to see if they were fully opened and whether they were even speaking to me. An era was over.

To have drawn bouquets,
full of life,
accompanied by a chorus of crickets,
what a privilege it was.

To a once-in-a-lifetime decade,
I dedicate this book.

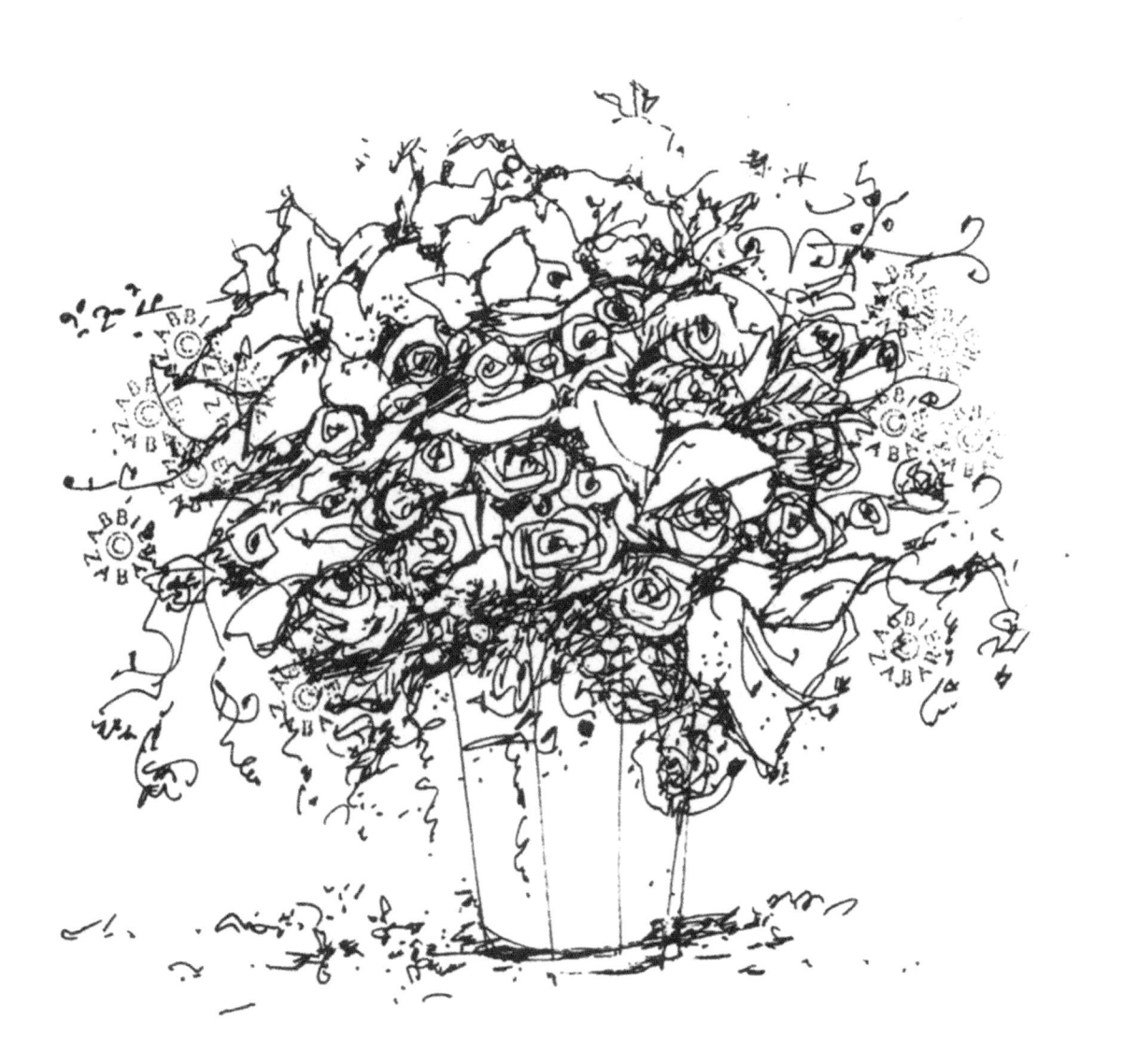

Acknowledgments

A bouquet of thanks to:

Alfonso Flores · Alicia Whitaker · Amy Goldman · Anna Gattani · Anne-Marie Colban
Barbara Ericsson · Ben Anayati · Brendan Kenney · Bryan Huffman · Chris Giftos
Chris McMahon · David Robinson · Dominick Corvino · Emily Evans Eerdmans
Ernie Cavallo · Harold Klein · Jane Lahr · Janee Ries · Janet Lobatt · Joel Ludlow
John Rommel · Joyce Davis · Kay Spear Gibson · Kevin Hogue · Laura Nagler
Liz Neumark · Lori Chips · Lyn DelliQuadri · Maria Josefina Meza · Mary Albi
Matt Mattus · Maureen Ryan · Michael Riley · Peter Hellman · Rob Stanford ·
Steve Whitesell · Tibor Hegedus · Vail Barrett · Valerie Raffle · Will Frece ·
Zeus & Zorro Zabar

ACC Art Books:
Alice Bowden · Andrew Whittaker · Corban Wilkin · Craig Holden · James Smith ·
Mariona Vilarós Capella & Stewart Norvill

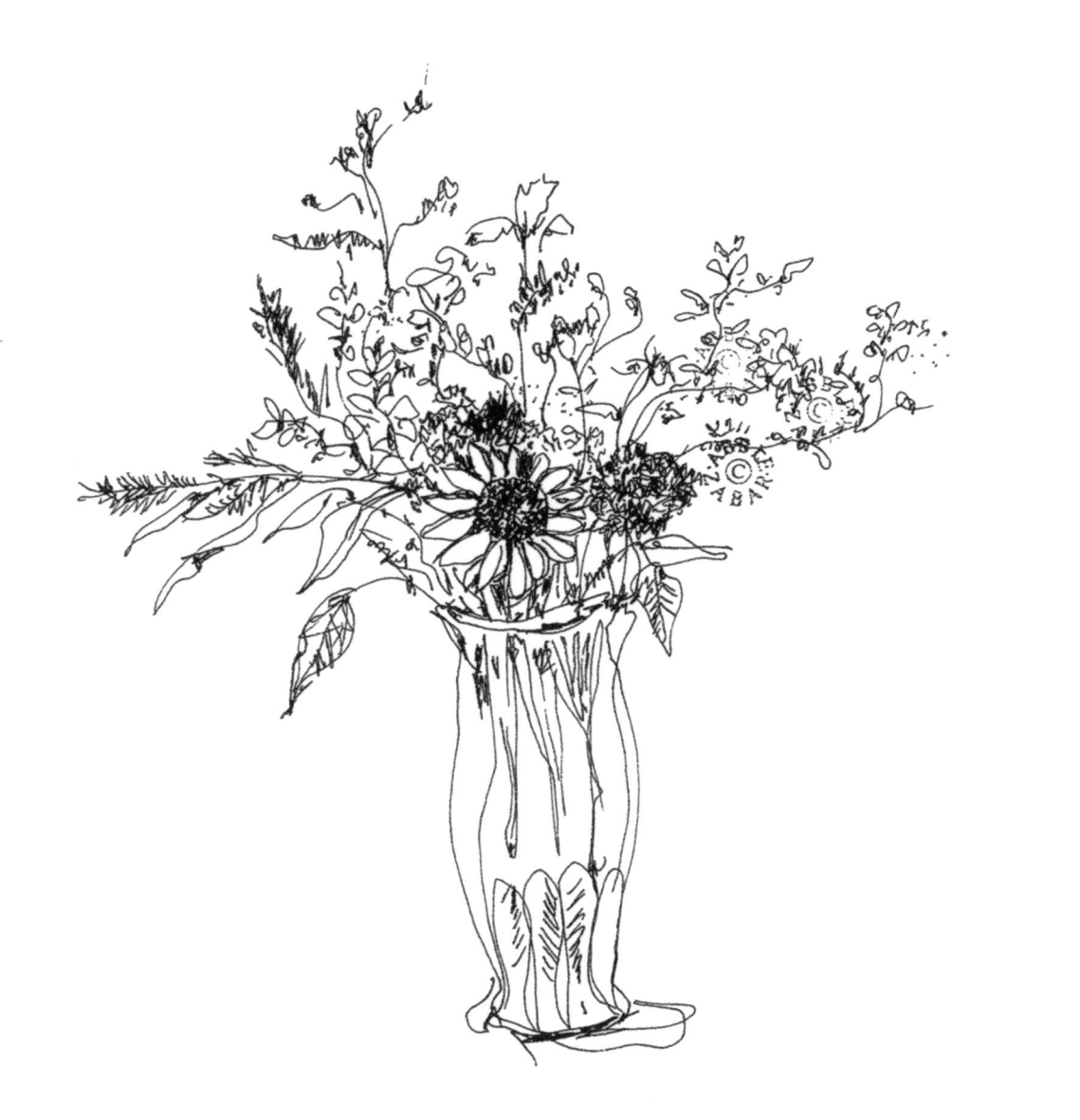

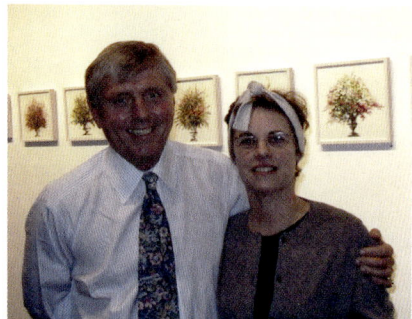

Chris Giftos and Abbie Zabar, 2000.

Frontispiece: Another bouquet in its niche.

p.6: New York's Metropolitan Museum of Art in miniature.

p.9: Going through the columns, from the Great Hall on the way to the ancient collections.

p.10: Red-hot pokers and droopy lobster claws of *Heliconia*, also called "false birds of paradise".

p.17: "Plate II against Page 110." Langley, B. (1728). *New Principles of Gardening: Or, The Laying Out and Planting Parterres, Groves, Wildernesses, Labyrinths, Avenues, Parks, &c. After a More Grand and Rural Manner, Than Has Been Done Before*. A. Bettesworth and J. Batley, London. Photo courtesy of Abbie Zabar.

The author and publisher gratefully acknowledge the permission granted to reproduce the copyright material in this book. Every effort has been made to trace copyright holders and to obtain their permission for the use of copyright material. The publisher apologises for any errors or omissions in the text and would be grateful if notified of any corrections that should be incorporated in future reprints or editions of this book

Editor: Stewart Norvill
Design: Mariona Vilarós Capella & Craig Holden
Reprographics: Corban Wilkin

EU GPSR Authorised Representative:
Easy Access System Europe Oü, 16879218
Address: Mustamäe tee 50, 10621 Tallinn, Estonia
Email: gpsr@easproject.com Tel: +358 40 500 3575

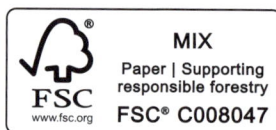

FSC
www.fsc.org

MIX
Paper | Supporting responsible forestry
FSC® C008047

Printed in China by C&C Offset Printing Co. Ltd for ACC Art Books Ltd, Woodbridge, Suffolk, UK

www.accartbooks.com

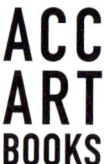

ACC ART BOOKS